Percy Thrower's
PICTURE BOOK OF
GARDENING

Percy Thrower's

PICTURE BOOK

OF

GARDENING

LONDON
W. H. & L. COLLINGRIDGE LTD

*First published in 1961
by W. H. & L. Collingridge Limited
2–10 Tavistock Street, London, W.C.2
Printed in Great Britain by
Harrison & Sons Limited
London and High Wycombe
© Percy Thrower 1961*

Fourth impression 1964

Contents

Foreword

I live for gardening; not only do I garden as a profession, but I make it my hobby as well. Of all hobbies today gardening is No. 1 for there are more people gardening for pleasure than doing any other single hobby we could mention. This I can easily understand for a garden can give so much.

It is estimated that there are approximately ten million people in this country with either a garden or an allotment. Of these almost one tenth are really keen gardeners. Another twenty-five per cent are interested and enjoy their gardens. About fifty per cent garden more or less because they have that piece of ground round the house and realise it cannot be left to grow weeds. The remainder do little or nothing with their gardens. How I wish they were all keen gardeners: how much more beautiful our cities, towns and villages would be, and how much healthier. Thank goodness interest in gardens and gardening is increasing rapidly. More and more people have a house with a garden, many of them for the first time.

A garden is a place in which we can enjoy many peaceful hours among our favourite plants, trees and shrubs, a place where we can forget the worries of the outside world. It provides a place where we can enjoy healthy exercise and relax at the week-ends and in the cool of the spring, summer and early autumn evenings. Perhaps of greater importance to many people, a garden will provide a wide variety of flowers for the home as well as fresh vegetables, salads and fruit far better than any we can buy. Is there any wonder that gardening is No. 1 hobby?

How is it possible to get all these benefits from our gardens? Firstly we must remember that we get from the garden only what we put into it, and that means effort, time and patience. The soil must be our first consideration. It is not just dirt but something which contains living organisms essential to keep the soil healthy and provide plants with necessary foods. We must endeavour at all times to keep the soil in good heart whether it be for flowers, fruit, vegetables or even for the grass on the lawn. This can only be done successfully by good cultivation, allowing air to penetrate the soil and by keeping it well supplied with humus in the way of manure, garden compost, peat, spent hops, leaves, lawn mowings, etc. Apart from providing plant foods the humus will retain a certain amount of moisture for use during dry periods and will improve the texture of the soil.

Moisture is the controlling factor in plant growth. The amount of growth our plants will make depends on the amount of moisture they are able to get. We can add to the moisture in the soil by watering and also by mulching on the surface to prevent evaporation.

We can provide extra plant foods by using the more concentrated fertilisers, those which contain the three essential plant foods most likely to be in short supply, namely nitrogen, potash and phosphate. We cannot keep on taking away the grass mowings from a lawn unless we put something back. In the autumn, the spring, as well as in the summer, the grass too needs these plant foods. We can only do this by top dressing in the autumn and winter and by using fertilisers in the spring and summer. A good lawn will set off the garden to its best advantage. If the soil is kept in good heart we shall get full value for the money we spend on fertilisers.

The gardener must at all times endeavour to keep his plants and crops free from insect pests and diseases. They cannot be healthy and grow as we would wish them to if they are attacked by greenfly and other insect pests sucking their sap or eating their leaves or if they are crippled by mildew or other fungoid diseases. There are these days many insecticides and fungicides to make our task an easier one.

The garden must be kept free from weeds. It is a well known saying among gardeners, 'One year's seed, seven year's weed', so weeds must be hoed off in the seedling stage and never be allowed to produce flowers and seeds. The hoe is the gardener's best friend. It should always be kept handy and whenever there are a few spare moments it can be used between the seedlings and other plants. I prefer the Dutch hoe, of which there are many kinds. This, pushed backwards and forwards just below the surface of the soil, not only chops off the weeds but at the same time stirs the surface of the soil and helps air to penetrate to the plant roots. Weeds compete with the plants, not only for plant foods but also for the necessary light and air. There is no place in a well kept garden for weeds.

How essential it is that we buy good seeds from a reliable source. Also, none but the best tools will do. They make our work easier, and if properly cared for will last a lifetime.

The edges of the lawn must be kept neatly trimmed, the hedges as well, and the garden will be a place of constant beauty, interest and relaxation throughout the spring, summer, and well into the autumn.

Another joy I find in gardening is that I never finish learning. I go into the smallest garden and see something I have never seen before or learn something new. I try to pass on that which I have learned throughout the many years I have been gardening, at the same time keeping it in simple terms that are easily understood even by the beginner. In 1948 I began a regular gardening programme on the B.B.C. radio. In those days it was necessary to build a word picture. With television we now have the visual aid and the picture is much easier to follow than one made with words alone. That I think applies in a book too and in this book I have endeavoured to keep the pictures as clear and concise as those on B.B.C. Television 'Gardening Club', with as few words as possible in the hope that I am passing on the enthusiasm that I myself have for gardening in general.

It is impossible to cover the whole field of horticulture in a book such as this and I can only hope I have chosen the most popular subjects which will be of value to the majority. I am told that 'Gardening Club' has nearly five million viewers week by week, many with gardens, some without. I trust this book will be of value to its readers and that they will get from their gardening the fascination and reward that I get from mine.

Shrewsbury, 1961   PERCY THROWER

Lawns

I suppose that one of the main features in nearly every garden in the country is the lawn. Practically every gardener plans to have a lawn and there is no doubt that there is nothing more restful than a smooth expanse of grass. We cannot all achieve lawns like bowling greens but we can go a long way towards that goal by making careful preparations beforehand and by regular maintenance thereafter.

Many people fail to remember that lawn grasses are plants which need feeding and looking after just like other plants. Failure to feed properly means that the finer grasses gradually die out and are replaced by the strong coarse grasses. There are a number of excellent lawn foods available and it is essential to keep the lawn weed free by applying one of the many weedkillers now available. But, apart from the application of proprietary fertilisers, any gardener can do much to improve the condition of his lawn by topdressing it each spring. Alternate layers of farmyard manure and good loam, stacked for a year or more and then screened through a fine sieve, makes a good topdressing. Other suitable mixtures are ordinary loam and peat, leafmould and peat and dried sewage sludge. These should be scattered evenly over the surface, about $\frac{1}{4}$ in. deep and worked into the lawn by hand or with the back of a rake.

It is often a good plan, when taking over a new garden, to put a good deal of it down to grass. Eventually, when time allows, flower beds can be cut out of the grass, and planted up as soon as they have been dug over, for if the lawn has been looked after they will be virtually free of pernicious weeds.

Many gardeners make themselves a lot of unnecessary work in mowing by having right-angle corners to the lawns and beds of rectangular, circular or oval shape. Much labour can be saved by arranging for all corners to be gently curved and for all beds to be of such a shape that you can mow round them easily without having to stop and back the machine. The simplest shape for this purpose is a long fish-like shape, without the tail fin. If you want to save labour, plan your beds in this shape.

No pathway should lead directly on to the lawn, unless it is continued in the form of stepping-stones sunk to the level of the turf for easy mowing. Where pathways lead on to the lawn you will have worn places which look shabby and constantly need renewing.

There is no need for a lawn to be absolutely level. A sloping lawn, provided the slope is gentle to allow for easy mowing can be very attractive.

Do not forget to trim the edges after mowing; nothing sets off the lawn like neatly trimmed edges.

PREPARING AND SOWING A NEW LAWN

Careful preparation of the site is essential. It may take a long time to do the job properly, but I can assure you that it is worth it in the long run.

The first job is to get the ground dug over thoroughly (1 and 2). I like to get this done in the autumn, as early as possible before the soil gets too wet. Then the soil can be left in rough clods for the winter weather to break up. Remove all the roots of perennial weeds as you go along. In picture 3 I am removing the roots of couch grass, a pernicious weed. Get every bit of this out otherwise you will have trouble later.

The action of the wind, frost and snow help to break up the clods and make it possible to get ahead with the next stage as soon as the ground dries out in spring.

Then it is a good plan to apply a dressing of a complete fertiliser (4); two ounces to the square yard is about right. Scatter it evenly all over the plot. Next I like to go over the plot with a fork (5), breaking down the clods. Watch out for any weed roots at this stage, too, and pick them out for burning.

The ground will need firming. The best way to do this is to walk all over it, feet together, treading down firmly with your heels (1). Then, using an iron-toothed rake, rake first one way (2), and then the other, removing all the larger stones and any weed roots. This will break down the smaller lumps of soil so that you should have a fine seed bed.

Choose a dry day in April and divide the plot up into strips a yard wide with garden lines. Sow your grass seed at $1\frac{1}{2}$ oz. to the square yard as evenly as possible (3), working close to the soil if it is windy. Then lightly rake it in (4).

If you want a fine lawn avoid mixtures containing perennial rye-grass. For a hardwearing lawn choose a mixture with 30% rye-grass.

If the weather is mild and damp the first blades of grass will appear about 10 days after sowing. Do not worry if weeds appear as most of these will disappear when regular mowing begins. Hormone weedkillers should not be used until the lawn is approximately 6 months old.

The first cut can be given 4 to 6 weeks after sowing but do not cut too closely. All that is necessary is to remove the tips of the leaf blades. Some people like to use shears for the first cut but this is only practicable on a small area. New lawns suffer more from drought than established ones and it is wise to water in dry spells.

LAWN MAINTENANCE

Established lawns need looking after to keep them in good condition. In late winter, when the grass is reasonably dry, sweep the lawn with a stiff besom to scatter worm casts (1), otherwise the flattened casts will leave ugly slippery marks and smother the fine grasses. Raking with a spring rake (2) will remove moss and dead grass.

To prevent the turf from becoming compacted it should be spiked all over each autumn. This can be done with a special machine incorporating a rake or spiked roller (3), with a special tool which removes plugs of earth (4), or with an ordinary garden fork (5). A topdressing of fine soil at about 4 pounds per square yard will feed the grass (6). Work this into the turf with the back of a rake.

14

A good method of widening a grass path is to lift the turf (1) at the edges to a width of 9-12 in. The soil is then forked over (2) and levelled to the desired width—a garden line will ensure a straight edge. The turf is then replaced by turning it around so that the neat and straight inside edge is relayed on the outside. Rolling with a light roller (3) will consolidate the turf. The gap that results between the two sections of turf, which can be seen in the top left picture, should be filled in with fresh soil and then sown with grass seed. The same procedure can be followed where turf at the edge of a path or border is ragged or uneven. Where it has sunk the turf can be lifted (4) and new soil filled in to correct the unevenness so that

when the turf is replaced it is level with the rest of the grass.

Repair work of this nature is best done in the Autumn as the turf can make new roots before the onset of hard weather. If left until the spring it may suffer in a dry spell unless watered very thoroughly.

It sometimes happens that hollows appear here and there in a lawn. This often occurs where the soil underneath was not evenly consolidated before the lawn was laid. The fault can be remedied easily enough by

15

lifting the turves in the affected area (1) and packing fine soil underneath until they are level (2). Finish with a light rolling.

Sometimes lawns become invaded by moss. This is destroyed by treating the grass with lawn sand (3) in dry weather. Afterwards rake out the blackened moss and resow with seed.

When lawn weeds are few it is wasteful to apply weedkiller all over the lawn. I use a special tool for spot treatment of the occasional weed. The weedkiller, in tablet form, is put in the cylinder (4) which is filled with water (5). The weedkiller is applied just where it is needed (6).

Where the lawn is badly infested with broad-leaved weeds you should, of course,

treat the whole area. The modern selective weedkillers are fine for this but they must be used carefully. The two main points to remember are to use them only at the rate recommended by the manufacturer and to do so only on a still day to avoid drift damage. I usually apply them with a watering can fitted with a fine rose (1). If there is the slightest hint of wind, delay using them, otherwise there is the risk of damaging nearby plants. It is a good plan to cover these with newspaper or sheets of plastic.

Lawns need mowing frequently in the growing season (2). If you mow while the grass is still short you may leave the grass box off as the clippings will soon wither. Vary the direction of mowing each time so that if you mow up and down one time mow across the next. Long-handled shears are useful for grass close to trees and shrubs (3). In the autumn sweep up all fallen leaves regularly (4) and store them in heaps to rot down (5).

MOWER MAINTENANCE

Properly maintained, your mower will give you years of faithful service. Oil it occasionally during the season. Scrape encrusted grass off the blades with an old knife (1). It also pays to wipe the blades over after use with an oily rag to prevent rust (2).

At the end of the season the mower should be given a thorough overhaul before it is put away. Clean and grease all parts and test the blades for sharpness with a piece of paper (3). Regrinding is a skilled job and the machine should be sent away. It is best to get this done early in the winter rather than in the spring, for then you may find the waiting list so long that it will be weeks before you get your machine back.

Until it is needed in the spring place the machine in one of those huge polythene bags and keep it in a dry shed.

Before use check that the bottom blade is not set too low. A straight edge laid between front and back rollers (4), will show the true height of the blade at a glance.

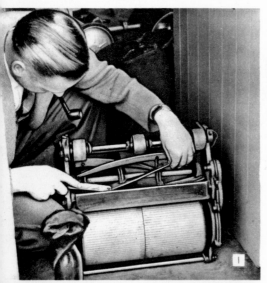

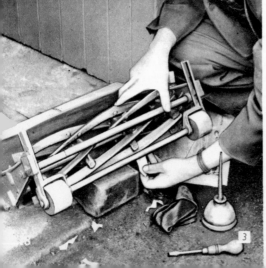

Flower Borders

I often think that there is more scope for the exercise of ingenuity in the design of flower borders than of any other feature in the garden. Shapes and sizes can be infinitely varied to suit the circumstances and as far as planting goes there are many thousands of plants from which to choose.

In our parks at Shrewsbury we have many flower beds of different kinds and we try to make them as colourful as possible for as long as possible for we know that they are appreciated not only by the townspeople but by the many thousands of visitors.

Without facilities for changing bedding plants rapidly the amateur gardener cannot, perhaps, arrange for such a continuous flowering season but if the beds are properly planned it is usually possible to have something in flower from early spring until late autumn.

For their main display many gardeners rely on a border of herbaceous perennials, for once these are planted not all of them need much attention except for routine staking and tying. Certainly it is possible to plan a good succession of colour in a border of this kind of reasonable size. If you are going to use the taller herbaceous plants you will want a border at least 6 ft. or 8 ft. wide but it is possible to plan narrow borders for quite small gardens, for there are many suitable low-growing plants available. Do not forget that it is best to plant in groups to get the best effect.

For quick results there is little to beat the annual border, particularly in a new garden. Such a border can be sown in March or early April and by July it will be a blaze of colour, continuing for many weeks, especially if the dead flower heads are removed regularly. There are scores of suitable hardy annuals available for these borders and if there is a greenhouse or cold frame available then the range is greatly extended for the half-hardy types can be grown, too.

In the Shrewsbury parks, as in other parks, we make great use of bedding plants, many thousands of which we raise annually for spring and summer display. It is possible, even in a small greenhouse or frame, for the amateur to raise many of these plants for setting out in late May or June. There is a great satisfaction in growing one's own plants in this way, although perfectly good results can be obtained from bought plants, provided some care is exercised in their choice. All too often these are on sale in April and, in my opinion, it is far too early to plant them out then, for cold nights will check them severely. Strong plants set out in late May or early June will quickly get away and will flower for many weeks.

I prepare my annual border by marking the positions for each kind in the soil with a stick (1). I then put labels in each space with the packets of seed to be sown there (2). The seed is sown in shallow drills (3) and after sowing a light raking covers the seed (4).

I always plant lilies in groups on a layer of coarse sand to provide sharp drainage (5).

Spring bulbs can look very charming planted in grass, especially if they are in informal groups. If you use a special tool which lifts out a plug of turf (6) all you do is to pop the bulb in, right side up, replace the plug and stamp on it.

DIVIDING PLANTS

It pays to divide such plants as Michaelmas daisies annually. I find that this produces stronger, larger spikes and the plants are less

liable to be attacked by mildew.

After lifting the clumps with a fork (1), divide them into small pieces (2), discarding the worn-out centres. As you can see, I prefer to use a trowel for replanting the pieces (3).

Montbretias are often neglected and the clumps fail to flower properly. It is best to lift the clumps every other year in February, split up the corms and replant them (4). The popular scabious also need dividing every second or third year in March. I just dig up the clumps and thrust two forks into the clump back to back and lever them apart until the clump splits (5). The old stems and dead leaves are then removed from the pieces (6). Replant the pieces in groups in well prepared ground that is not short of lime (7).

Early April is a good time to take cuttings of such plants as herbaceous phloxes, delphiniums, lupins and heleniums. Cut off the young shoots near the crown and dibble them into sandy soil in a deep box (1) covered with a sheet of glass. Water them and shade them from bright sunshine.

After they have finished flowering, overgrown clumps of flag irises can be lifted (2), divided and replanted. Split the rhizomes up into pieces containing a sheaf of leaves (3). Trim the leaves and when replanting (4) do not bury the rhizome (5).

Border carnations are best planted a foot apart in October or March (6). In June go over the plants and disbud them, reducing them to one bud on each shoot (7).

When planting herbaceous plants do not forget to label them (1).

A mulch of peat round established plants will keep the ground moist, keep down weeds and eventually improve the texture of the soil (2).

I like to feed plants in the herbaceous border each February. The ideal is to spread a layer of rotted manure or compost all over the surface, but this is not always

available. However, a good general flower fertiliser will help a good deal. This is sprinkled round the plants (3) and then forked in (4).

Early flowering plants such as Christmas roses benefit from a similar feed in summer (5). Sprinkle this all round the plant and lightly fork it in. Then, in November, when the buds appear (6) it is worth placing a sheet of glass (7), or cloche over the plants to bring them along in time for Christmas and protect the beautiful white flowers from being splashed with mud when it rains.

You will get better flowers from many herbaceous plants if you thin out the stems. Cut out surplus stems (1) and stake and tie those that are left (2).

Other herbaceous plants are best supported with twiggy pea-sticks (3).

Tall bedding plants such as the crimson *Lobelia cardinalis*, sometimes need staking. Thin canes are unobtrusive (4).

You can prolong the flowering of many plants by cutting off the flowered stems as soon as the flowers have faded. This will also prevent the plant from wasting its energy on ripening seed. Cut down lupin spikes as soon as they fade (5).

In late autumn tidy up the border by cutting down all dead stems (6). In cold districts red-hot pokers should have their leaves tied up for protection (7). A ring of ashes round delphinium crowns will protect young growths from slugs (8).

The Rock Garden

There are few of us who have not admired the beautiful jewel-like flowers one sees growing in rock gardens. Rock gardening, like growing chrysanthemums or dahlias, is just another specialised form of gardening, one which attracts many gardeners because there are so many delightful plants which can be grown in this way. Rock gardens can be quite small, using a few pieces of stone, covering a few square feet, in which many diminutive plants will flourish, or they may be very extensive with immense rocks and large pockets of soil, in which big plants including shrubs are grown. Fortunately, there is such a wide range of plants that there is no difficulty in finding suitable ones for gardens great or small. And, although the main flowering period is in the spring, it is possible by choosing plants carefully to have something in flower for practically every week of the year, even in a quite small area.

However, a rock garden is not merely a haphazard collection of pieces of rock or lumps of concrete, sticking up at all angles, with pockets of soil in between them in which dwarf plants languish. A properly constructed rock garden should, as far as possible, look like a natural outcrop of rocks and give the impression that the rocks seen above the surface are far fewer than those that lie beneath—like an iceberg, which has most of its bulk below water level. To give this impression it is not necessary to have enormous lumps of stone—the quite small pieces I am seen handling on the next page are sufficient although if they are available one or two large pieces are helpful to provide the keystones around which the rock garden is built.

To get this naturalistic effect it is best to use stone with well-defined lines or strata. Water-worn Cumberland limestone and certain hard sandstones are the best. Granite and marble are the most unsuitable types. The rocks are laid so that the strata lines run approximately in the same direction. Although this is easier when you build the rock garden on a bank, many successful gardens have been built on the flat. Try to ensure that the garden is built in a series of rough steps and this will leave pockets of soil behind each layer to accommodate plants. These can be filled with lime-free soil compost for lime-hating plants, peat for peat-lovers etc., or you can put in deep beds of gritty soil for those that like sharp drainage. But ordinary loamy garden soil will do for most alpine plants. Crevices left between the rocks can be used to plant alpines which will create a natural effect. As the plants are supplied in pots it is possible to plant at almost any time of year.

Be careful when moving heavy rocks into position or you may injure yourself. For really large ones it is necessary to use a block and tackle and boards.

BUILDING A ROCK GARDEN

The small pieces of rock I am seen handling here are quite sufficient in size to form a pleasing rock garden. You will see that I am laying them to give the impression of natural lines or strata mentioned on the previous page. I am pointing to the strata lines to indicate which way they run in picture 4. For each rock the soil must be dug out (1) and it should be tilted slightly upwards at the front (3). To prevent wobbling the soil must be carefully packed behind and around each one (2) to ensure that there are no air pockets into which roots may penetrate and die.

The pieces of stone should be laid to look as natural as possible. This is difficult with oddments and it pays to buy a load of suitable material particularly if there is a quarry in the neighbourhood.

After the rock garden has been completed it is a good plan to topdress the soil. Where you are growing lime-hating plants peat makes a good topdressing (1). In fact peat can be used for all plants as it helps to retain moisture and is gradually absorbed into the soil to improve its consistency. If the natural soil is on the heavy side coarse sand can be worked in with a handfork (2 and 3). Where the natural soil is poor it is best to remove it and replace it with a prepared compost of fibrous loam, moist peat and coarse sand.

Planting between the rocks must be done carefully with a small trowel or handfork (4). Make sure that the soil is firmed evenly.

There are numerous small shrubs and conifers suitable for a rock garden. These are best planted first. Do not plant too closely as many alpines spread rapidly.

As alpines are often grown in pots in the nursery it is safe to plant out pot-grown plants (1), even while they are in flower. This will give you a quick display. Shade the plants for a day or two from strong sun.

Many alpines can be propagated quite simply either by lifting and dividing the plants or by detaching rooted offsets. Cuttings of others root readily if small pieces are detached (2) and dibbled into pans of sandy compost (3). After they have been watered (4) a pane of glass is placed over the pan (5) and it is put either in a cold frame or in a shady place outdoors until the cuttings have rooted. Wipe condensation away from the glass each day and when the cuttings have rooted pot them separately in 3 in. pots using a compost containing coarse sand to ensure good drainage.

DRY WALLS

Dry walls are useful for separating one part of the garden from another or as retaining walls. They are carefully constructed, without cement between the layers of stone. Retaining walls should have a slight backward slope to provide better support. Earth should be packed in solidly behind them as they are built and construction will be easier if layers of soil are put between each row of stone.

As the stones are irregular in shape there will usually be spaces left between them for planting alpines (1 and 2). Aubrietas, alyssums, houseleeks, saxifrages and erinus look delightful planted in the face of the wall.

Alpines can also be grown in steps (4) which connect one garden level with another. Campanulas, cranesbills, sedums, thymes and the wall plants mentioned above are suitable. Holes can be left for plants when the steps are built but if this was overlooked it is not difficult to make holes large enough for the plants with hammer and cold chisel (3).

It is worth going over rock garden plants to cut off dead flowers (1). In the autumn dead leaves from nearby trees collect in the crevices between the rocks, blown by the wind. These should be removed regularly (3) otherwise they get wet and soggy and may kill the plants they are covering.

Some shorter growing lilies are fine plants for the larger alpine garden and it is easy to make up pockets of special soil for them. But they need staking against wind damage (2). The stems can be tied loosely with soft string or raffia. The canes are soon hidden as the plants grow up.

Some delicate rock plants such as lewisias and those with hairy leaves, such as the well known Edelweiss, survive cold damp winters better if they are protected with a pane of glass (4). This can be supported over them on four short sticks and kept in place with a stone. Instead, a cloche can be put over the plants.

Dahlias

The dahlia is such a variable plant that it is no wonder that in the last 150 years or so, since the dahlia was first introduced, it has become an immensely popular flower. Nowadays there are many different types ranging from the small pompons, with flowers less than 2 in. across, to the large decoratives, which have flowers at least 8 in. across, and in height from the dwarfs, about 6 in. tall, to the giants which may reach 5 or 6 ft. But it is in the shapes and formation of the flowers that the greatest variation occurs. So great is this variation that there must be dahlias for everyone. The man who hates the large decoratives with flowers like dinner-plates, will probably grow the delightful pompons with their symmetrically overlapping petals or the beautifully formed fancy types. The man who is too busy to attend to the plants very much can still get a good display of colour by growing the dwarf bedding types which need little attention other than deadheading.

It is quite easy to grow dahlias of a sort, in fact, it is possible to plant them in the cutting bed and leave them to look after themselves except for staking, and they will produce plenty of flowers. But you will not produce the best flowers by this method. Many of them will be short-stemmed, some will have distorted or weak-necked flowers and it is extremely unlikely that any will be up to show bench standard.

To do them well you have to give dahlias a deep, rich, well-dug soil, containing plenty of moisture-retaining material such as rotted manure or compost, because the plants need large quantities of water to make good growth. They grow rapidly from May onwards and need frequent feeding with liquid manure, and they benefit from a deep mulch round the plants both to provide food for the roots near the surface and to conserve moisture.

Stake the plants firmly quite early in their growth, using stout stakes. Dahlias are leafy plants and their stout hollow branches are easily damaged by wind. In order to get long-stemmed, well-shaped flowers it is necessary to remove side shoots and disbud soon after the flower buds have formed. Blooms required for exhibition purposes will need some extra support in the form of thin canes or wire loops and they should be shaded from the weather by some means, either semi-permanent screens or temporary dunce's cap shades fixed to separate stakes.

For ordinary garden display, of course, one need not take so many pains, although it is always worth going to some trouble to obtain good blooms.

The large-flowered decorative type of dahlia (1), which is of interest mainly to exhibitors, has flowers at least 8 in. in diameter. Cactus types (2) and pompons (3) are very useful not only for garden decoration but also as a flower for cutting. The large-flowered pompon dahlias have flowers 3 to 4 in. in diameter, medium pompons 2 to 3 in. in diameter and the small pompons have flowers not over 2 in. in diameter. Anemone-centred dahlias (4) are unusual and as they grow only 15-18 in. tall are useful for bedding out.

In the small decorative dahlias (1) the flowers are fully double and the petals are more or less flat. The bedding types (2) are free-flowering kinds and usually less than 2 ft. tall. Collerette dahlias (3) have one or more rings of flat outer florets (petals) surrounding a collar of smaller florets about half their length.

33

Dahlias are usually propagated from cuttings. The dormant tubers are placed in boxes of moist potting soil (1). When young shoots are about 3 in. long they are cut off with a sharp knife below a joint (2). The bottom pair of leaves (3)

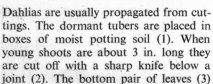

are stripped off and the stem trimmed cleanly immediately below a joint (4). The ends can be dipped in hormone rooting powder and the cuttings are then put in small pots containing moist cutting compost (5). When all cuttings have been inserted they should be watered (6).

Cuttings strike readily given bottom heat. As soon as they have rooted pot them on, handling them gently (1). Harden them off before planting out in late May or early June.

Dormant tubers may be planted out in late April or early May (2). By mid or late July it will be necessary to thin out the shoots to prevent overcrowding (3).

Plants will need staking. It is best to use four stakes or canes per plant (4). String wound from one cane to the other, cat's cradle fashion, will provide support (5). From mid July onwards feed the plants (6).

Some disbudding will be necessary, although I do not bother about this with the small-flowered varieties used for garden decoration. With large-flowered kinds and those needed for exhibition, except small pompons, where large flowers are not required, I disbud to retain one flower only per stem (1).

When frost threatens in early Autumn go over the plants and pick all remaining flowers (2). After frost has blackened the haulm cut plants down to a foot from the ground, ensuring that the remaining stem is labelled (3). Lift tubers a week or two later, working well away from the stem (4). Dry them off and dust them with flowers of sulphur before storing them in dry peat, sand or polythene bags in a frost-proof place (5).

Gladioli

Gladioli must be numbered among the favourite flowers of summer. The breeding that is going on all the time has resulted in the introduction of many fine new varieties in recent years, although some of the old-stagers are still going strong. Perhaps the greatest advance in recent years has been the introduction of the butterfly and other miniature types, less formal in appearance than the large-flowered kinds and much smaller both in total height and in size of flower. The development of these newer types has made the gladiolus a much more versatile plant, for although the large-flowered kinds can be used to make magnificent floral decorations, there is no doubt that they can be a little overpowering in small rooms.

There are fewer varieties of miniatures and the butterflies available so far, but those kinds that are on the market cover a fair range of colour, usually a ground colour striped, blotched or flushed with another colour. In the delightful miniatures the flowers are often heavily ruffled or crinkled.

In addition to the types mentioned so far there are, of course, the primulinus hybrids which more and more people are growing for their charming hooded flowers, refined in shape and colour. The individual flowers, although a little larger than those of the miniatures, are again smaller than the large-flowered hybrids, usually some $2\frac{1}{2}$ to $3\frac{1}{2}$ in. across, according to variety.

Because of its rather stiff formality the gladiolus is somewhat limited in its use for garden decoration. Where space allows, the plants can be grown in groups of half a dozen or a dozen behind other, earlier flowering plants to hide some of the stiffness of the gladiolus leaves. Gladioli have their uses in the herbaceous border, too, for they flower in late summer at a time when the summer flowers in the border have begun to go over and before the autumn flowers are in full bloom. In the border the large-flowered types are best, and should be planted in the middle row, in groups of half a dozen or a dozen. For cutting purposes there is no better place for them than in the kitchen garden. There, if gladioli corms are planted at intervals of a fortnight from March to May, they will provide a long season of spikes of bloom for the house.

Gladioli are not difficult to grow. If the soil can be enriched before they are planted, with rotted manure or compost, they will give better results, although if the ordinary soil is a good loam it will be suitable without further enrichment, unless the spikes are wanted for exhibition. It pays to lighten heavy soils with coarse grit and sand and to make light soils more retentive of moisture by adding moist peat. It is also worth while planting the gladioli corms on a layer of sharp sand where the soil is heavy, both to provide a little extra drainage and to make it easier to lift the corms in the autumn.

Although the miniature, butterfly-flowered and primulinus types of gladioli are gaining rapidly in popularity, the prime favourites are still the large-flowered hybrids. Scores of excellent kinds are available of which Antarctic, a beautiful white variety (1), is but one example. Note the length of spike and the number of flowers open at once.

The miniature, such as Bo-Peep (2), are beautiful little plants with ruffled and crinkled petals.

Primulinus types, a representative of which is shown at (3), are distinguished by the hooded flowers. Individually the flowers are much smaller than those of the large-flowered kinds but they are much daintier in appearance and are ideal as cut flowers.

Apart from these types there is a spring flowering kind called *G. colvillei*, which is mainly grown under glass for early flowers. There are not many varieties but The Bride with pure white flowers and Peach Blossom, a pink variety, are two that are popular.

Gladioli corms can be planted from March onwards until May to give a succession of flowers. Use a trowel and set them about 4 in. deep and 6 in. apart (1) in groups for display or in rows for cutting. Canes should be put in position quite early (2) so that no time need be wasted in tying the flower spikes in position as they develop (3). Use soft string or bast for this. Cut the spikes early, as soon as the bottom florets begin to open (4) and place them in deep containers of water for a few hours before arranging them.

Thrips are small slender insects that

cause a white mottling of the foliage and petals. At the first signs of attack spray with DDT or malathion.

In the autumn lift the corms carefully (5), dry them off, then pull off the dead stems (6) and break off the remains of the old corm (7). Store the corms in labelled bags in a dry frost-proof place. Save the cormlets. Sown like seed in rows outdoors they will soon produce flowering size corms.

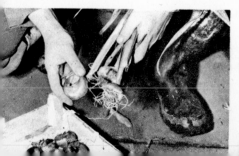

39

Sweet Peas

Sweet peas are favourites with many gardeners. And deservedly so for they are among the most fragrant of all plants and produce so many flowers that from a well-grown double row a dozen feet long it is possible to pick several thousand blooms during the summer and early autumn.

One often sees sweet peas grown as a temporary hedge in cottage gardens, up twiggy pea-sticks. This method is quite satisfactory but the gardener who wants blooms of exhibition standard, long-stemmed with large, well-placed and well-formed flowers, will undoubtedly grow them by the cordon method. This means a good deal more work but the results are well worth it.

Grown by the cordon method the preparation starts well before the plants are set out. The first outdoor job is to prepare a trench 1½ to 2 ft. wide and 2 ft. deep. Into the bottom of this is forked 2 or 3 in. of well-rotted manure. The trench is then filled up to within 2 in. of the top with good loamy soil. If this is not available use your ordinary garden soil mixed with organic material from the compost heap.

Before the seedlings are planted out in April the canes are put in position. These are strong bamboo canes 7 or 8 ft. long, set 6 to 9 in. apart.

As soon as the plants start growing all tendrils and sideshoots must be nipped out to keep each plant to a single stem and as the plants will have had their means of support removed they must be tied in regularly to the canes. When they reach the top of these you can carefully untie the plants, lay them along the ground and then start them on their upward climb again, up canes several feet away. This will keep them down to a reasonable height for picking, otherwise they might easily grow to a dozen feet or more in height. Before you start laying the plants remove all flower stems, otherwise they become damaged. New ones will form quickly.

In dry weather it is worth spraying the plants with clear water when the sun is off them and it is essential to go over the plants each day removing all spent blooms. Mulch the soil around the plants to conserve moisture and to provide additional food. Water very freely if the ground becomes dry. Feeding can be done with liquid cow manure or a well balanced fertiliser may be used. For best results sweet peas must be fed at regular intervals.

A few good modern varieties include Flaming Beacon, a bright orange scarlet; Mauve Princess; Pink Princess; Madame Butterfly, a delicate pink; Silver Cascade, a pink flushed lilac; Swan Lake, the best of the white varieties; Riviera Blue and Stylish, both large-flowered blue varieties, and Carlotta the best of the carmine kinds.

Apart from the tall growing sweet peas there are, also, dwarf bushy types such as the Cuthbertson Cupid sweet peas, which grow about 3-4 in. high and 12 in. across, and Little Sweetheart sweet peas. These grow a little taller and may need some twiggy sticks for support. They are excellent for the front of a flower border or for window boxes.

Late autumn is a good time to sow sweet peas in pots in a cold greenhouse or frame. Five or six seeds should be sown in each small pot of J.I. Seed Compost (1). By January the young plants will have made plenty of root growth and can be carefully divided up (2) and potted individually into 3 in. pots of J.I. Potting Compost (3). Give the plants some small twigs for support at this stage (4). Keep them cool at all times, a frost-free frame is quite sufficient. Sturdy plants will be produced for planting outdoors in April.

Another method of raising sweet pea seedlings is to sow the seed individually in soil blocks. These are easily made in the potting shed with the aid of a soil block press.

Small models are available at moderate prices. One seed is sown in the depression in the top of the block (1) and covered with a little more J.I. Compost (2). The blocks are packed in boxes (3) and they must be kept moist but not overwet. The tips of the seedlings should be removed (4) when the second pair of leaves has formed. The great advantage of this method is that the seedling stays in the soil block and grows steadily until it is ready for planting out (5), thus minimising root disturbance.

To do sweet peas well they need a lot of organic material in the soil. It is best to dig a trench for them (6) at the bottom of which can be placed quantities of rotted manure, compost, hop manure or any other organic material.

If it is possible, take out the trench in the autumn or winter (1) and leave it exposed to the effects of the frost and weather. Plant out in early April in the south but planting can be delayed until May in the north. Set the plants out 9 in. apart either in single rows or in double rows with 12 in. between them. Use a trowel for planting (2). If you grow the plants cordon fashion on single stems, get the canes in at planting time. Build a stout framework of canes to withstand wind (3). As plants develop remove all side-shoots and tendrils (4). When the plants reach the top of the supports the stems can be lowered and retrained up canes further along the row (5).

Chrysanthemums

Few flowers add so much colour to the late summer and autumn garden as the chrysanthemums and there are not many flowers that are so valuable for garden display and for cutting for the house.

The fact that the chrysanthemum is a variable plant has led to its unending development in the past hundred years, since Robert Fortune sent home from Japan in 1861 a number of Japanese varieties. Development in more recent years has been along the lines of producing better and better incurving and reflexed varieties, although such kinds as the anemone-flowered and rayonnante types are finding much favour nowadays.

The main types, grown in large quantities, both by amateurs for exhibition and for cutting purposes and by the trade for cut-flower sale, are the types with tightly incurving florets (petals) making a globular flower; the incurving types which are looser in formation; the reflexed in which the petals bend back, and the anemone-flowered. However, every type and class (and there are 25 sections in the National Chrysanthemum Society's classification) has its enthusiasts.

The early-flowering outdoor types are very popular, but to give of their best they need constant attention. For this reason they are usually grown in formal rows. There are, however, several outdoor kinds which will provide plenty of late summer and autumn colour without much attention and these can take their place in the herbaceous border if necessary. They are the Korean hybrids, the rubellums, the Lilliput varieties and the singles, all colourful plants, suitable either for the front or the middle of the border, requiring much the same sort of cultivation as most border plants.

The chrysanthemum is a plant which responds to good cultivation. The aim should be to produce a fertile top-spit of soil by digging and incorporating moisture-retaining materials. We all know how short is the supply of well-rotted farmyard manure and we have to fall back on substitutes these days. Well-made garden compost is a good substitute and spent hops are sometimes available. Peat retains moisture if dug in when thoroughly damp, but it does not supply plant food. However, it can be used successfully if the deficiency is made up with a well balanced general fertiliser. There are very few soils that cannot be improved by this treatment. On the heavier types of soil it helps to scatter basic slag on the surface at 1 lb. per square yard after the winter digging has been done, when the compost or manure substitute is dug in. About a month before planting, the plot should be forked over to break down the lumps. A dusting of bonemeal through the soil at this stage will provide some slowly-released plant food.

The aspect is not really important, but the site chosen for chrysanthemums should be an open sunny one, well away from hedges and trees, although a hedge between the plants and the quarter from which the prevailing wind blows will do much to lessen gale damage.

Although many more gardeners are finding that they can get much pleasure out of having a greenhouse, it is not at all difficult to grow outdoor chrysanthemums without one. The plants are hardy enough to survive the winter in a completely cold frame, although it is wise to throw mats or sacks over the lights in very severe weather. Otherwise the plants can do with plenty of ventilation and soil on the dry side, especially in colder weather. It is possible to raise the temperature in the frame in late winter and early spring by lining it with polythene sheeting. This will bring the plants along a little more quickly, enabling cuttings to be taken from them in late February and early March. The cuttings can be rooted in a small propagating frame, placed inside the main frame. Rooting will be somewhat slower in these conditions but strong young plants should be ready for planting out from mid-May onwards. The main thing to avoid in frame culture is over-watering which will result in a sodden soil. Lack of ventilation and dampness are the ideal conditions for the spread of damping off diseases.

When the plants are set out they can either be grown in rows or in small groups in the border. Whichever method is adopted the plants will need staking and tying properly to prevent wind damage. To get the best blooms the plants must be stopped and disbudded at the right times, according to variety and the grower's experience. It is worth keeping your own notes about this so that you can refer to them each year.

Various pests and diseases are liable to attack chrysanthemums and a regular spraying with such insecticides as nicotine, malathion, BHC and DDT will be needed to ward off pest attacks. An occasional spray with a fungicide will keep mildew at bay. It is particularly necessary to spray with insecticide in late summer and autumn to deal with the destructive attacks of earwigs. Before housing the stools in frame or greenhouse dip them in an insecticidal bath and treat all cuttings and young stock in the same way. Virus diseases can be very destructive but nowadays heat-treated stocks, free of certain viruses are available. I should give a word of warning about these. Properly treated stocks are invaluable, but they should be obtained from chrysanthemum specialists. It is not practicable for the amateur to treat his own stocks as the high temperature that must be maintained and the skilled attention that is needed are beyond his resources. Although treated stock may be free of some destructive viruses, it can readily become reinfected unless aphids are kept under control with malathion, BHC, or nicotine.

Incurved (1) and incurving (2) chrysanthemums are two of the most popular types. An incurving variety has flowers with petals that incurve loosely in contrast to the tightly arranged petals of the incurved kinds. Reflexed types (5) include varieties with outward pointing or drooping petals as well as kinds with reflexed outer petals and incurving inner petals. Pompons (3) have dainty small flowers and the true singles have a centre disk and not more than five rows of outer florets (4). Apart from these main types of outdoor chrysanthemums there are also the Korean and Charm kinds.

46

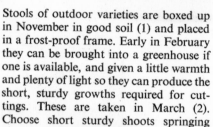

Stools of outdoor varieties are boxed up in November in good soil (1) and placed in a frost-proof frame. Early in February they can be brought into a greenhouse if one is available, and given a little warmth and plenty of light so they can produce the short, sturdy growths required for cuttings. These are taken in March (2). Choose short sturdy shoots springing

directly from the roots and after removing the bottom leaves trim them off just below a joint, using a sharp knife or razor blade (3). Dip their ends in hormone rooting powder (4) and insert them, half a dozen to a pot containing cutting compost (5). Make sure that each cutting is well firmed and label each pot (6) with the name of the particular variety.

The rooted cuttings are potted on into individual 3 in. pots (1), hardened off in a frame and planted out in late April or early May. Prepare the ground beforehand, digging it deeply and incorporating some well-rotted manure or compost. The plants should be set out 1½ to 2 ft. apart in rows 2 ft. apart and put stakes in beforehand. Knock the plants gently out of their pots with the handle of a trowel (2), plant with a trowel (3) and give the plants a first tie (4). Stop the plants about mid-May by pinching out the centre growing point of each plant (5). This will cause the plant to branch and as new growths develop more ties will be needed (6). From July onwards the plants will need feeding with a good general fertiliser. Scatter this round the plants (7), hoe it in and if the weather is dry water thoroughly to wash it into the ground.

Growths will need constant tying to prevent wind damage (1). By late July it will be necessary to disbud (2) unless you are growing the plants to provide sprays. If large flowers are required, or if they are needed for exhibition, I leave one flower bud to each stem, removing all the surrounding buds and side growths to leave a clean stem. It is safer to leave the buds until they can be handled easily. Premature disbudding may result in damage to the crown bud.

As the flowers develop they will need some protection from the damaging effects of wind and rain. Bags, held on wire frames (3) are ideal for this.

After the flowers are over the plants can be cut down to a few inches from the ground (4). Make sure that they are labelled properly. Lift them in mid-November (5), place them in boxes, cover the roots with soil or peat (6) and place them in the frost-proof cold frame until they are needed for cuttings. During the winter very little water will be needed and every effort should be made to avoid a damp stuffy atmosphere in the frame. In these conditions fungus troubles can develop. The frame light should be opened during the day whenever possible to allow a free circulation of air.

Roses

I cannot help thinking that roses are the most rewarding of all plants. Provided one can manage to give them a minimum of attention in the way of pruning, the hybrid teas and floribundas will go on happily year after year, producing magnificent crops of blooms from late May or early June until the winter comes to put an end to their blooming. Admittedly, not all classes bloom perpetually and with some of the old-fashioned kinds and some ramblers the season is fairly short by comparison. But even so they are worth growing for few flowers are so worthwhile in their season.

Although roses are not demanding in their requirements, like many other plants they really give of their best when they are properly looked after. They are not very fussy about soil; the only kinds they really seem to dislike are the thin soils overlying chalk. Yet even these are capable of improvement by the addition of organic matter. It is a fallacy, of course, to say that roses prefer heavy clay. They grow very well on the heavy clay soils but these must be thoroughly dug first. Once the clay has been broken up the roses will flourish but it is as well to dig in a fair amount of organic material such as rotted strawy manure or garden compost to improve the texture of the soil. Some sort of plant food is essential on any soil for the bushes will be in active production for many years. Much can be done by feeding and mulching the bushes annually, but this cannot take the place of thorough preparation before planting.

By choosing the right kinds of roses it is possible to find one for every purpose. For formal rose gardens the standards, half-standards and bushes are ideal. For shrub gardens and for less formal situations there are many fine shrub roses, including the 'old-fashioned' kinds, which are usually heavily fragrant in flower and some are decorative in fruit. Many of these shrub roses require little if any pruning apart from the removal of dead or dying wood and left to themselves they make large bushes. For gardens large enough to take them I would recommend the spinosissima hybrid roses raised in Germany by William Kordes. These include Fruhlingsgold and Fruhlingsmorgen, both of which grow 6 ft. tall and bear very large single or semi double roses.

For walls, pergolas, fences, pillars and arches roses reign supreme. The climbers, the climbing sports of the hybrid teas or the wichuraiana hybrids, all have their place and will give good accounts of themselves if pruned properly each year. With the true ramblers it is best to cut away the old flowered shoots entirely after the flowers have faded, and tie in the long new shoots which will have been produced. With the climbing hybrid teas it is necessary to prune carefully lest they revert to a non-climbing habit. Thin out the old flowered shoots after flowering is over, go over the plants in spring and cut out dead wood and thin, weak shoots and tip the remainder.

The hybrid tea roses with their large flowers, of which a good example is shown at (1) are still the most popular of all bush roses, although the floribundas (2), with smaller flowers in clusters, bid fair to equal them in popularity as more and more varieties are introduced. The climbers (3), including the climbing hybrid teas and pernetianas and the ramblers (4) of both the wichuraiana and multiflora types, are fine plants for walls, pillars, rose arches and trellises.

PLANTING AND PRUNING

Rose planting can be done at any time between October and March except in dead of winter. If the ground is not ready when the roses arrive plant them temporarily in an odd corner until they can be planted permanently. Protect the roots from wind and sun with sacking (1) while you are digging the planting hole. Make this of sufficient size so that you can spread the roots out properly. Shovel a little soil round the roots (2) and firm it with your boot heel (3). Repeat this until the hole is filled. Keep the point of union between stock and scion just below soil level. After planting prune the bushes back hard to within 6 or 8 ins. of the ground (4). Established bushes do not need such hard pruning (5).

The stronger growths can be cut back in March to five or six buds (1) and any thin, weaker ones to two or three buds or removed entirely together with the dead or dying wood (2). Always prune back to an outward pointing bud and do not cut too close to it. The result should be an open bush (3). The pruning of established floribundas is less drastic but differs little. Strong, young stems are pruned lightly (4) and older stems and dead snags are cut back hard or removed entirely (5). Aim to leave a bush as shown at (6). Always use sharp secateurs for pruning. If they are blunt, ragged cuts will be made, the stems may be torn and the pruning wounds will heal slowly. A bad cut may also cause die back of the shoot.

July dressing of a general fertiliser containing plenty of potash (5) will help the bushes to produce their second crop of flowers. Suckers can be a nuisance so they should be removed right back to the root (6) as soon as they are seen. If they are cut off at soil level this will result in a crop of new suckers.

Shorten flowered side growths of climbing sports (1) and keep the new growths tied in (2). A light dressing of basic slag (3) can be given advantageously in winter and a spring mulch (4) will provide food, improve the soil and keep down weeds. A

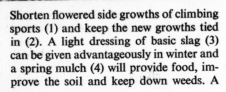

Spray regularly with BHC or malathion (1) to prevent attacks by greenfly and other pests. I like to go over the bushes in the autumn and half prune by cutting back the flowered stems (2). To grow roses on their own roots take cuttings with a heel of older wood (3) in early September.

Trim the heels and remove the lower leaves (4). Dip the ends in hormone rooting powder and insert them for half their length in narrow trenches with sand or vermiculite at the bottom (5). Firm them well after setting out (6). Refirm the soil in winter around cuttings that have become loosened by frost.

Bedding Plants

In the parks at Shrewsbury we make great use of spring and summer bedding plants in order to ensure a continuity of colour from spring until the frosts kill the half-hardy annuals. Although amateur gardeners are unlikely to go to great lengths to change the bedding schemes regularly throughout the summer as Parks Superintendents do, it is certainly worthwhile going to some pains to provide a good range of bedding plants especially if a greenhouse is available for bringing up the more tender plants.

As far as colour goes the bedding season starts in spring with the daffodils and wallflowers, the forget-me-nots and tulips, the hyacinths and stocks, the polyanthus and coloured primulas and the dwarfer plants such as alyssum, arabis and aubrieta. When these have been cleared away their places are taken by the summer bedding plants, of which there is a great variety. Those that are popular include the snapdragons, the double-flowered begonias and the *B. semperflorens* hybrids, the Canterbury bells, fuchsias, heliotropes, lobelias, nemesias, zonal and other pelargoniums, penstemons, salpiglossis, salvias, stocks, sweet williams, French and African marigolds, verbenas and zinnias.

Where it is desired to have a continuous scheme of bedding, work goes on for most of the year. Late in January or early in February in the warm greenhouse seeds of half-hardy and tender plants are sown. In March many plants need stopping to induce a branching habit and softwood cuttings of heliotropes and verbenas are taken. In June, when the early summer bedding is beginning to flower it is time to sow seed outdoors of biennials such as wallflowers and Canterbury bells and in autumn cuttings of ripe growth are taken and tender plants are stored for the winter.

Bedding schemes can be varied endlessly. In large areas it is possible to plant up elaborate designs, using carpeting plants of different colours, combined with low-growing edging plants such as lobelias, ageratums or sweet alyssum, with taller-growing dot plants such as standard fuchsias to give added height and to relieve monotony. Many such intricate schemes are seen in big public parks and municipal gardens. But there is no need for such elaborate schemes in private gardens, where space is much more limited. There the simple designs based on the rectangle, circle or oval and using fewer different types of plants are perfectly effective. Wallflowers, tulips and forget-me-nots can be followed by snapdragons, edged with ageratums and interplanted with petunias. One must, however, be ruthless where these schemes are concerned. At the end of May when the summer plants should go in, the wallflowers are often still in full bloom. But they must be discarded, together with the forget-me-nots, and the tulips must be lifted and heeled in temporarily elsewhere until their foliage has turned brown.

hand (4) and scatter seeds thinly on the surface of the compost (5). Cover them lightly by sieving soil on to the surface through a greenhouse sieve. This can be made up by removing the bottom of a box and replacing it with perforated metal. Try to apply the sifted compost evenly by shaking and moving the sieve up and down the box (6).

SEED SOWING

Prepare the box by covering the drainage slits with crocks and filling with John Innes Seed Compost (1). Make sure the compost in the corners is well firmed (2) and finally firm with a wooden firmer (3) to provide an even, smooth surface. Shake some of the seed out into the palm of your

prick them out (5) into boxes of John Innes Potting Compost. Space them out well. Hold the seedlings by the leaves only. Never hold a seedling by its stem as it is very delicate. A normal seed box can take nine rows of five or six seedlings. A simple way of labelling boxes is to pare one edge with a knife (6).

Water the box, using a fine rose (1), place a label in it (2) and cover with a sheet of glass and a folded sheet of newspaper (3). Keep the box in the warmth and turn the glass every day to wipe away condensation. As soon as the seeds have germinated remove glass and paper and when the seedlings are large enough to handle (4)

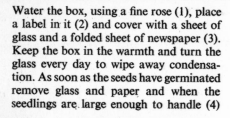

Smear white paint along one edge (1) and write the name on this (2). Water the seedlings (3) and keep them out of strong sunlight for a day or two after pricking out. Instead of pricking them into boxes they can be pricked out into individual soil blocks. Hold the seedlings gently by

one leaf, fill the hollow with soil (4) and gently firm with the fingers (5).

Afterwards the soil blocks can be put close together in seed boxes stood on the greenhouse staging. The outside of the blocks tend to dry out quickly and watering must be attended to regularly.

The usual time for sowing wallflower seeds outside is in late May or early June. Prepare the seed-bed first by breaking the soil down with a fork and then firming it by treading. Afterwards rake over the site to obtain a fine tilth and then take out shallow drills, a foot apart. In dry weather these may have to be watered (1) before the seed is sown thinly (2). Label the rows with the name of the variety as they are sown and cover the seed by shuffling soil over them

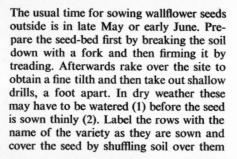

with the feet (3). When the seedlings are through dust the rows with DDT against flea beetles (4). These are small insects which can puncture holes in the seed leaves and in a severe attack the seedlings may be destroyed. It is easier to work between straight drills so use a garden line when taking them out and sowing.

In a few weeks, usually by the second half of July, the young seedlings must be transplanted to a nursery bed. This should be of good soil, in an open sunny situation. It is not wise, however, to plant wallflowers in soil that is rich in nitrogen. This will encourage the plants to make soft, sappy growth which is likely to suffer in the winter.

A dressing of sulphate of potash to the soil at 1 oz. per sq. yd. will help to produce sturdy growth. Set the plants out 9 in. apart in rows 9 to 12 in. apart to enable you to hoe between them easily (1). In early October they will have made bushy plants and must be lifted (2) and moved on again to their flowering quarters. Firm the plants with your foot (3) as you plant them and go over the beds after frosts and high winds to refirm them. Hoe between them (4) to keep down weeds.

(1). Plant them in their flowering positions in October.

I start taking cuttings of bedding geraniums in August. By looking carefully over the plants in flower it is possible to find firm, sturdy unflowered shoots about 6 in. long (2). These are collected and brought back to the greenhouse and prepared for rooting by cutting off the bottom leaves close to the stem (3) and then trimming the cutting immediately below a leaf joint (4) with a sharp razor blade or knife. A number of clean 5 in. pots are crocked and then filled with a suitable gritty cutting compost (5). Notice that I have close at hand all the necessary materials and equipment, such as hormone rooting powder, water in which to dip the ends of the cuttings, pots, boxes and compost.

Winter-flowering pansies, attractive plants which are used for spring bedding or for spring display in dry walls as they come into flower in March, are sown in June in boxes in a cold frame. In August they can be pricked out on to a finely broken down nursery bed, spacing them 3 or 4 in. apart

1

3

2

(4) and place them on the greenhouse staging. The cuttings should root quickly but look over the pots regularly and remove and burn immediately any cuttings that are developing black stems (5). At the same time remove dead leaves (6). To avoid rotting of the stems water the cuttings sparingly, particularly when temperatures are low.

After covering the cutting compost with coarse sand (1), to assist rooting, I insert the cuttings round the edge (2) after dipping the ends first in water, then in rooting hormone powder. After firming the cuttings with my fingers (3) I water the pots

4

6

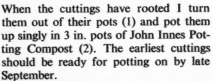

When the cuttings have rooted I turn them out of their pots (1) and pot them up singly in 3 in. pots of John Innes Potting Compost (2). The earliest cuttings should be ready for potting on by late September.

Heliotrope cuttings (3) will root easily in a propagating frame. When rooted pot them individually (4). Cannas must be lifted before the frosts. I divide up the roots with a sharp knife (5), cut their foliage back and pot them up (6) for wintering in a frost-free greenhouse or frame. The plants rest in the winter and very little water need be given at this time.

Centaurea gymnocarpa, the silvery leaved foliage plant, is very useful in bedding schemes. It is a half-hardy perennial sub-shrub, growing about 1½ ft. tall and it is invaluable for toning down the hotter colours of such plants as the scarlet salvias, and small groups of well-grown plants look very effective by themselves.

Quite large pieces of the plant will root if they are taken in mid-September. Pieces are removed from the plant (1) with a heel of older stem attached. The heel is trimmed (2) and the lower leaves removed. To make sure that a large percentage of the cuttings will strike the ends of the cuttings are then dipped in water (3) and in hormone rooting powder (4). Half a dozen of them are then inserted round the edges of 5 or 6 in. pots of sandy cutting compost (5). Each cutting should be firmed well and afterwards the pots are watered (6).

This plant can also be raised from seed sown in a heated greenhouse in March. Use John Innes seed compost and when large enough prick out the seedlings into boxes; transfer later to 3 in. pots. Plant out in the open in early June.

In a warm shaded part of a greenhouse (1) the cuttings will soon root. When they have formed good roots they can be turned out of their pots (2), divided up (3) and potted singly (4).

Polyanthus plants grown from seed, sown in February or March, are ready for putting out in May or early June. Choose a partially shaded bed and set them out in rows (5). Established plants can be divided after they have finished flowering (6) and the pieces replanted in a shady bed until required for planting in their flowering beds in the autumn.

In October clear away the summer bedding plants (1) fork beds over (2), tread the soil to firm it (4) and tidy it up with the rake (3) ready for replanting. Winter flowering pansies (5) and polyanthus are useful for a narrow border and they can be lifted in early October from nursery

beds. If polyanthus plants have produced flower stems remove these on planting (6).

Polyanthus can be grown permanently in a shaded border provided the soil is good. They should, however, be lifted and divided occasionally otherwise they are likely to deteriorate.

It is best to plant with a trowel (1) making a hole large enough to accommodate the roots comfortably (2). Firm the plants well with the knuckles (3) and after planting prick over the soil between them (4) to remove footmarks in which water might collect and to leave a neat appearance. Go over the plants again after severe frost to refirm them where necessary.

Polyanthus and primrose flowers suffer badly from attacks by birds in the spring. You can do much to prevent this by stretching black cotton or nylon thread over the beds (5) on stout canes a little taller than the flower stems.

SUMMER BEDDING

After the spring bedding plants have been cleared away the beds are again forked over and a good dressing of bonemeal or a general fertiliser worked into the soil. I tread the soil over (1) to firm it and then start marking out the positions of the various plants. When dealing with large beds I find it helps to use a large pair of compasses (2). The first plants to set out are the dot plants such as *Centaurea gymnocarpa* (3). The main groundwork such as salvias is put in next (4). These are spaced out evenly all over the bed. It is always best to plant with a trowel. As you can see from the photograph these salvias were reared in soil blocks. I find that this method means that there is far less root disturbance on planting.

There are, of course, a great many other plant combinations for a colourful display in summer. Standard fuchsias and standard geraniums are useful with a groundwork of bedding dahlias or coloured leaved geraniums.

1

Keep the hoe going between bedding plants (1) to destroy weeds. In dry weather it may be necessary to water, especially plants such as fuchsias (2) which need a good deal of water. Where the beds are

2

surrounded by grass, neat edges set them off properly. After the grass is mown trim the edges (3). To keep the beds neat it is sometimes necessary to trim plants that wander over the edges (4).

4

3

HANGING BASKETS

Hanging baskets, filled with summer flowering plants, are very decorative when hung from convenient points such as a porch or from long brackets on a wall. Among the best plants for such baskets are the ivy-leaved pelargoniums and the fuchsia. Cuttings of both these plants can be taken in late summer. Cut off short pieces of the ivy-leaved pelargonium (1), trim each cutting below a joint (2), remove the lower leaves and insert the cuttings in pots of cutting compost (3). Short lengths of fuchsia can be removed in the same way (4), the flowers removed (5), stems trimmed and the cuttings inserted in pots (6) where they will soon root. The young plants can then be put individually in 3 in. pots of J.I. compost and kept in a light and cool greenhouse.

Hanging baskets can be made up in April and kept in the greenhouse until late May or early June when they can go outside if necessary. Line them thickly with moss (1) and fill them with potting compost (2), setting some plants in through the wires to trail as you do so. Firm as you go along (3) and set the plants in at an angle (4). Always keep the baskets well watered (5) and if fuchsias are grown it is wise to feed them each week in summer with weak liquid manure. Train some of the more flexible stems to the wires with hairpin-like pieces of wire.

Other suitable plants for hanging baskets include pendulous begonias, *Asparagus sprengeri*, *Campanula isophylla* and variegated nepeta.

Garden Pools

A garden pool, however small, can be one of the most attractive features in the garden. Such pools are not difficult to construct in concrete, and once the edges of this have been disguised with plants or paving slabs, it does not look nearly such a harsh substance.

Nowadays it is possible to buy pools, formal or informal, already made in fibre-glass and plastic. These are available in various sizes and shapes and it is only necessary to dig a hole to receive them. The edges are disguised with flat paving stones. Pools have also been made successfully in recent years using heavy-grade polythene sheeting. The method is a simple one. A hole of the right shape and size is dug and the bottom and sides beaten flat, taking out any sharp stones in the process. The polythene sheeting is placed in position and a little water run in to hold it in place. Then the edges of the sheeting, which should overlap the pond edges by a foot, are folded under and held in place with flat paving stones. The pool can now be filled, although planting is done most satisfactorily when pools are empty.

Many plants such as water-lilies and other aquatics are best if planted either in beds on the bottom of the pool or in baskets which are weighted with stones. In any case it is best to plant in a fibrous, turfy loam. Water-lilies are available for pond depths of less than a foot to $2\frac{1}{2}$ to 3 ft, and when ordering make sure you get the kinds suitable to your pond. But in addition there are other suitable plants, including the Water Hawthorn, The Water Violet, the Golden Club and floating plants, such as Frog Bit and Water Soldier. If you are going to have fish in the pond you ought also to have a few oxygenating plants. These help to provide oxygen for the fish and, although they are often referred to as water-weeds, they are a necessary part of the pond planting scheme.

Much of the beauty of the pond comes from the plants which surround it, growing either in very shallow water a few inches deep, actually on specially made ledges, or in boggy soil near the edge. Here can be planted various irises, the Flowering Rush, Marsh Marigolds, single and double, Sweet Flags, *Lobelia cardinalis*, Bog Bean, Arrowheads and the ornamental rushes and reed maces. For the sides of larger pools a spectacular plant is *Gunnera manicata*, with huge leaves 4 to 6 ft across. In moist, but not waterlogged soils you can plant astilbes, day-lilies, hostas, *Iris kaempferi*, lysichitums, lythrums, mimulus, many moisture-loving primulas, spiraeas and trollius.

Fish and water snails will help to keep the water clean and will provide a good deal of interest in themselves. Breeding pairs of goldfish and shubunkins are not expensive. In some districts it may be necessary to take precautions against herons by stretching nets below the surface of the water.

It is occasionally necessary to remove surplus oxygenating weed such as blanket weed. This can be done with a rake or fork.

PLANTING A POOL

One way of planting a water-lily is to make a special bed for it on the bottom of the pool. Pieces of stone can be used (1) to make the bed which is filled with good fibrous loam (2) in which the water-lily is planted (3). A few stones over the top (4) will hold the soil and plant in place. Less elaborate planting is needed for such oxygenating plants as elodea. A rubber band placed round the root ball (5) is sufficient to hold it together. It is then placed at the bottom of the pool. Water is run in gently from a hose (6). Blanket weed can be removed from the water with a fork (7) or a rake.

Trees and Shrubs

The beauty of most gardens is enhanced by planting flowering or foliage trees and shrubs or ornamental conifers. But apart from their own beauty these plants are, to some extent, labour-saving plants, for once they are planted many of them need little attention beyond an annual pruning and some of them do not need even that. Eventually, when well developed, the shrubs help to keep down weeds.

The modern shrub garden is a far cry from the dull Victorian shrubbery. Since those days many new shrubs have been introduced from Asia and other places and the worth of many of the older shrubs has become increasingly recognised. Even in quite small gardens it is possible by careful choice to have shrubs in flower all the year.

Flowering shrubs are being used increasingly in conjunction with herbaceous plants to form mixed borders in which the shrubs help to provide continuity of colour and also give form to the border in the winter. Many shrubs make fine wall plants and given the shelter of a warm wall it is often possible to grow kinds which might more easily be cut by frost in more open situations. There are some small trees that make excellent lawn specimens and a good many shrubs which are ideal for clothing rough banks. Some will thrive on chalky soils, others demand peaty conditions; in some the flowers are followed by ornamental fruits, others are grown for the beauty of their autumn leaves. In fact, there are shrubs or trees for every soil, site or purpose.

In the following pages I have described briefly the cultivation of some of the more popular shrubs and trees but they represent but a few of those available and I would refer readers to catalogues issued by the specialist nurseries.

There are a few general points about cultivation that are worth noting. The main point, perhaps, is that, since shrubs remain in the same place for many years, unlike most herbaceous plants, it is essential to prepare the ground well. If a full scale shrub border is planned then the ground must be dug over deeply and as much rotted manure or compost incorporated as can be spared. This soil preparation is particularly essential for shrubs or trees to be planted and trained against walls as the soil at the foot of a wall is often very poor and dry. Planting holes should be large enough and deep enough to accommodate the roots without cramping. Trees and large shrubs need staking against the wind. Use stout stakes and put them in before planting. Make several ties and protect the stems as shown on page 77.

A summer mulch of leafmould or compost provides food and keeps down weeds. Even if no pruning is recommended it is always worth going over the plants occasionally with secateurs to remove dead and dying wood. There are few really serious pests and diseases and what there are are usually controlled quite easily with the normal insecticidal and fungicidal sprays.

When planting a tree in grass I remove the turf first (1). I make a hole amply big enough to accommodate the roots (2) and dig it over deeply. The soil that is removed is put onto sacking laid out nearby. The next job is to put a stout stake into the centre of the hole, hammering it in firmly (3). It must be put in the ground before planting. If it is left until later the roots may be damaged. The top of the stake should come a little below the point where the branches develop, otherwise the stake may chafe on the branches. All this time the roots of the tree have remained bagged up to protect them from drying wind and sun. Now they are undone and the tree placed upright in the hole, tied to its stake temporarily and its roots well spread out (4). I then return the earth a little at a time round the roots, firming it as I go along (5). As the soil is returned and before it is firmed, the tree can be moved up and down to allow the soil to trickle into the spaces around the roots.

The rest of the soil is then tipped from the sheet of sacking around the tree (1). After this the tree must be firmly tied. I first put a roll of sacking round the stem (2) to prevent it from chafing. Instead of sacking you can use sections cut from old motor tyres, or pieces of old hose-pipe slit down the middle. The tree and stake are then tied together firmly, twisting the string between tree and stake (3). Two ties are necessary for tall trees to make sure the wind cannot rock them. The ties must be renewed each spring. The stem of a young tree swells rapidly and unless the ties are replaced there is always a danger that they will cause restriction. Instead of using string and sacking adjustable ties can be purchased which may be loosened as and when necessary. I always think it gives a good finish to the job to cut round the edge of the hole again with the spade (4). I like to finish off the surface with a thick mulch of leafmould or peat.

Some shrubs are best set out when they are small as they dislike being moved too much. It is much easier to establish ericas if they are planted when young. October is a good month to plant them. Heathers can be obtained to give a succession of flower right through the year. *Erica darleyensis*, for instance, starts to flower in November and goes on all through the winter months, and *Erica carnea* is usually in bloom by Christmas. Holes sufficiently large for these small shrubs can be made with a trowel (1), but make sure that they are planted firmly, using your heel for firming if possible.

An effective grey-leaved shrub, easily raised from cuttings in a cold frame, is *Senecio laxifolius*. Cuttings can be taken in July or August and when they have rooted (2) they can be potted up individually (3) and (4) and the pots left in the frame or stood in the open until the plants are large enough to set out in a nursery bed.

Phlomis fruticosa, a shrub with yellow flowers, can be treated in the same way and when large enough to lift (5) they can be planted out in their permanent quarters. When planting shrubs it is not sufficient merely to make a hole, put the roots in and then return the soil and stamp on it. The

hole should be wide enough and deep enough to accommodate all the spread-out roots without doubling them up, or the whole of the root ball if the roots are balled. The hole I have made (1) for this well-grown *Senecio laxifolius* is big enough to allow for future root development. I return the finer soil round the roots first (2), shake the plant to allow the soil to trickle around the roots, and firm it with my heel (3).

Before planting rhododendrons or azaleas I add a bucketful of peat to the hole (4), add more peat round the root ball, firm the plant (5) and finish off with a good mulch of peat all round the plant (6). To keep the roots cool and moist apply a good thick mulch of moist peat, compost or spent hops around the shrubs each spring (7).

There are few soils on which hydrangeas naturally turn blue, but it is usually possible to ensure that they have flowers of this colour by treating the soil around them with a special hydrangea colourant. The best time to do this is late in July to ensure that the following year's flowers are blue. The powder is scattered all round the bushes (1) at the rate advised by the manufacturer.

I prune established bushes of hortensia hydrangeas in the spring, cutting off last year's dead flower heads (2) left on during the winter to protect the new buds from frost damage. These flowered shoots should be cut back to a well developed pair of buds. At the same time I remove dead and any thin straggly growths.

Hydrangeas are sometimes attacked by red spider mites but these can be controlled by spraying with malathion, taking care to spray the undersides of the leaves (3).

After rhododendrons have finished flowering it is wise to go over the bushes and remove the remains of the flower (4), to prevent seed forming. Snap out the old flower heads carefully, to avoid damage to the developing buds round them.

The copper-leaved hazel (*Corylus maxima atropurpurea*) is a fine foliage shrub which requires a certain amount of pruning. In early spring I go over the plants cutting out the older stems entirely (5), together with any dead and weak wood, to encourage strong new growth.

The purple-flowered *Buddleia davidii* (1) is a shrub which can be pruned drastically each spring, almost down to the ground (2) if necessary. Old bushes, too, can be cut back hard (3 and 4). Strong new growth will result which will flower later in the summer.

The popular, golden-yellow, spring-flowering *Forsythia spectabilis* (5) should be pruned immediately after it has flowered. Cut the shoots that have flowered back to young side-shoots (6) and thin, weakly shoots (7) back to their point of origin. Retain strong young growths for future flowering.

The yellow-flowered winter jasmine, *Jasminum nudiflorum,* is one of the best of all winter-flowering shrubs. Its leafless stems are wreathed in flowers from November or December onwards for many weeks. It is especially suitable for training against south or west walls (1), although in sheltered places it may be grown in the open. Established bushes make a mass of whippy growths and these should be pruned after the flowers are over. Train in any that are needed for covering the wall and reduce the rest to three or four buds (2).

The hardy, or nearly hardy fuchsias, such as *F. magellanica* and *F. m. riccartonii* (3) are sometimes cut by frost. The growth can be cut back almost to ground level in February (4) and new growth will spring from the base. There are several beautiful hardy hybrids, such as Mrs Popple and Uncle Charlie, which can be treated in the same way.

Caryopteris clandonensis (1) is a fine blue-flowered, late summer shrub. Pruning is very simple. Merely cut back the stems to within a few inches of their base (2) in March. They soon make a mass of new flowering growths.

Hydrangea paniculata grandiflora bears immense conical heads of creamy-white flowers (3) from July onwards. You can either leave it unpruned to make a large bush with smaller flower heads or prune it hard in late February, cutting it back (4) like *Buddleia davidii*.

The golden-yellow stems of *Salix vitellina* are among the most colourful sights of the winter garden. To ensure a plentiful supply the shrub should be cut hard back in spring (5).

Brooms (cytisus) are apt to get leggy if not pruned. Shoots that have flowered can be cut back after flowering (6) but not into old wood.

83

The sweetly-scented mock oranges, of which Sybille (1) is a good form, are among those shrubs which are best pruned after they have flowered to make them produce new growth for flowering in the following year. Cut back the growths that have flowered to a young shoot (2). Other shrubs that can be treated in this way are weigela and kerria. Heather, too, can be pruned after flowering, either with secateurs (3) or trimmed over with shears. This helps to keep the plants neat and compact and new young growth soon develops. *Pyrancantha lalandii*, one of the firethorns, a fine berrying shrub for a north wall (4) is best pruned in April or after flowering. The system is to shorten the long, side growths (5) in order to keep the bush in shape. It is possible to trim it back even closely against the wall but this results in loss of berries. When this shrub is grown in the open little pruning is needed.

Variegated hollies are beautiful ever-

greens. They may be left unpruned or
kept in shape by pruning or clipping them
between May and July (1). Many trees
produce suckers or unwanted 'feathers'
from the main trunk. Cut the growths off,
close to the trunk (2). Clematis of the
jackmanii type need to be pruned hard
each year. Each growth can be cut back
to one pair of buds from its base (3) in
February. Treat those of the *lanuginosa*
and *viticella* groups in the same way.
Prune *C. montana* after flowering, removing some of the old growth. Thin out
the growths of the *florida* and *patens*
groups in February. Yucca (4) make fine
specimens. Cut off the flower stem (5)
after the flowers have faded. It is worth
lightly forking over the soil in the shrub
border in autumn (6) to aerate it.

HEDGES

If hedging plants arrive when the weather is too bad to plant them heel them into a trench, covering the roots with soil (1). Plant in late autumn or early spring, when the ground has been thoroughly dug over and cleaned. Incorporate some well-rotted manure or compost at the bottom of the site and scatter bonemeal through the soil. I use a straight edge as a guide when planting (2). The hedging plants here are the popular oval-leaved privet and after they have been set out and firmed they should be cut back to half their height (3) to induce them to bush at the base. Trimming can begin in the early stages (4) and at first the hedge should be kept low to thicken up the base. Afterwards it can be allowed to go to the desired height. When clipping keep the face of the hedge flat (5) and trim the top neatly (6).

Beech makes an excellent hedge. Set the plants out 12 to 15 in. apart (1), firming them well with your heel (2). A double staggered row of quickthorn, 8 in. apart, with 15 in. between plants (3) will quickly make a dense, impenetrable hedge. A useful attribute of beech is that if it is kept closely trimmed (4) in July, it will retain its tan-coloured leaves throughout the winter. For a true evergreen hedge I prefer *Chamaecyparis lawsoniana*. Cuttings of this can be taken in September in a sandy frame. A year later they can be lifted from the frame (5), potted up individually (6), firming the plants with the fingers (7), until they have made sufficient growth and a good root system for them to be planted out at 2 ft. intervals to form a hedge (8). The time to trim hedges of Lawson Cypress is in May or June, but if hard cutting back is necessary, this can be done in April.

PROPAGATION OF SHRUBS

Many shrubs can be increased quite easily. Heathers can be layered by taking out the soil round them to form a shallow bowl, pressing the shoots back against the sides and filling up the centre with peaty soil (1). Shoots with a heel of older wood can be detached from such shrubs as pyracanthas (2) in the Autumn. These are prepared by removing the lower leaves (3) and trimming up the heel (4). The ends are then dipped in hormone rooting powder (5) and inserted round the edges of pots of cutting compost (6). The pots are then watered (7) and placed in a cold frame.

The attractive *Euonymus japonicus albo-variegatus*, with its leaves variegated with white, can be propagated in much the same way as pyracantha. The shoots with heel attached are broken off from the plant in late summer (1), trimmed up (2), their ends dipped in hormone rooting powder (3) and then either put in a special outdoor cutting bed or in a cold frame. A good cutting compost should contain a fair proportion of coarse sand and a suitable mixture consists of 1 part sifted loam, 2 parts moist peat and 3 parts coarse sand.

Some shrubs with long pliant growths, such as rhododendrons, can be layered quite easily. The great advantage of this method is that the layer, which will eventually make a new plant, remains attached to the parent plant while roots are forming. The method is to cut a 'tongue' in the stem at the point where it is to be bent to the ground, by slitting it part through (4). It is then bent down, the cut edges dipped in hormone rooting powder, until it touches the soil. It is best to make a special little bed of light, gritty soil at this point. The shoot is held in place with a stout piece of wire (5) bent like a double hook. The end of the shoot is then tied to a short stake (6) to keep the shoot growing upwards.

After the layered shoot has been pegged down and its end tied to a stake, mound some more gritty soil over the part that is pegged down (1). If some peat is mixed with this it will retain moisture better, but in any case it is as well to water the ground round the layered shoot in dry weather. The layers of many other shrubs quickly form roots; it is often possible to find shoots that have layered themselves naturally where they have rested on the soil. But those of rhododendrons usually take much longer and it is often two years before sufficient roots have formed to enable the layer to be detached. It is then an easy matter to cut the shoot off on the side nearest the parent plant, dig it up and replant it.

The layered shoots of some shrubs often make fine root systems (2) with a mass of young shoots. It is often possible to divide them up, as I am dividing this *Viburnum fragrans* layer (3) into several new plants.

Willows are among the easiest of all plants to root. All that it is necessary to do is to cut up the stems into short lengths (4) in the winter and set them close together in rows in the open ground. They have been even known to form roots when put in upside down. Privet cuttings will root easily if taken in the winter. After frost it is a good plan to walk alongside the rows of cuttings (5) refirming them after the frost has raised them. It is usually possible to plant them out after they have been in the cutting bed for a year. Other flowering shrubs that can be propagated in this way from hard wood cuttings are flowering currants (ribes), Mock Orange (philadelphus), deutzia, *Buddleia davidii*, forsythia, kerria and *Cornus alba*.

Fruit Garden

No properly planned garden is complete without a section devoted to fruit, however small it is. Even in quite small gardens, where it is impracticable to grow top fruit such as apples, pears, plums and cherries, it is usually possible to find space for a few soft fruit bushes, currants, gooseberries and the like, or a row or two of raspberries. Such plants as loganberries and other hybrid berries can often be accommodated in a corner of the garden, trained up poles or along fences. And, in gardens small or large, there are always walls and fences against which it is often possible to grow trained trees, either such kinds as apricots, peaches and nectarines, which benefit from the extra shelter and warmth of the position by the wall, or fan-trained specimens of apples, pears, plums and cherries, both sweet varieties and morellos. Another opportunity for growing fruit in all types of garden is in the form of a fruit hedge, not perhaps along the roadside where the fruits are too obviously a temptation to small boys, but to divide one part of the garden from another. Such dividing hedges or screens are all too often planted up with the ubiquitous privet, whereas they might just as well be planted with apples or pears in either cordon or espalier-trained forms.

In recent years several nursery firms have put on the market the 'family trees' and these are ideal for the small garden in which there is room only for, say, one apple tree or one pear tree. They are available with three different varieties of dessert apples or pears grafted on them, or with two dessert and one cooking variety.

One point should be borne in mind when you are considering ordering either apples or pears. Varieties are available which are grafted on to dwarfing stocks and these are the types, in the form of dwarf pyramids, or dwarf bush trees, which are most suitable for small gardens. One of the most usual stocks for this purpose is known as Malling IX and trees worked on to this stock will come into bearing in two or three years so that there is the minimum of delay after planting before you can start enjoying the fruit. A dwarfing stock is available, too, for pears and trained trees are usually worked on to what is known as Malling C stock, which means that the trees will not get unduly large. Plum trees are often worked on to common plum stock and many varieties make good trees, that do not grow too large, on this stock. There is, unfortunately, no dwarfing stock available yet for cherries and this fact makes them unsuitable for small gardens as they are normally grown as standard or half-standard trees. However, good crops can be obtained by training cherries in fan shapes against walls and this has the added advantage that the trees can be more easily netted as the fruit is ripening as a protection against birds which often take the larger proportion of the crop from trees grown in the open.

As I have mentioned on page 119, when discussing vegetables, the amateur fruit grower has a great opportunity of growing the best varieties, not all of which are grown commercially for sale in the shops. Cox's Orange Pippin, Worcester Pearmain and Bramley's Seedling are the kinds of apple grown most often by the commercial grower because these are the kinds that the housewife has come to know best and ask for in the shops. But there are many other fine apple varieties well worth growing which are never seen in fruit shops. This applies, too, to other kinds of fruit.

One of the amateur's biggest headaches in fruit growing is caused by the question of pruning. But, once the various principles are understood, this is not a difficult operation. Many people are inclined to prune too hard, not realising that this forces the tree to produce a mass of new growth, much of it unwanted, which has to be pruned away again later. The main objects of pruning are to form the tree to the desired shape; to improve the quality of the fruit and to regulate the yield of fruit year by year. Subsidiary, but still important objects, are to get rid of dead, dying or diseased wood and to keep the bushes or trees open so that light and air can get at them to ripen both the fruit and the new wood that is developing and on which fruit will be borne in the years to come.

Unless maiden, that is one-year-old, trees are purchased, the initial pruning and training will have been done by the nurseryman, whether the tree is intended to be a standard or half-standard, a pyramid, a bush or a fan-shape. Thereafter part of the pruning must be directed towards maintaining this shape by the removal or cutting back of unwanted or straying growths. The other main objective will be to force the tree into forming fruit buds or new growth on which fruit buds will develop. This usually happens anyway as a consequence of using the knife or secateurs. Some kinds of fruit trees, such as cherries and plums, do not take kindly to pruning and are pruned as lightly as possible to keep them in shape and to remove dead or dying wood. On the other hand, some bushes such as blackcurrants must be pruned drastically to make them produce new fruiting shoots.

In the following pages I have described the cultivation of a number of different fruits and given directions for pruning. I have not attempted to discuss varieties as these are very numerous indeed where some fruits are concerned and I would suggest that the reader consults the catalogues issued by specialist nurserymen.

When planting fruit trees I like to put a stout stake in place first. A short stake only is needed for this bush tree (1). I then spread out the roots after tying the tree to the stake temporarily (2). I work fine soil down among the roots by shaking the stem while filling the hole. I add more fine soil, a little at a time (3) and firm with my heel (4). I then replace the temporary tie with a permanent one, placing a roll of sacking round the stem (5) to prevent it from chafing against the stake. The tie must be inspected from time to time to make sure that it is not too tight.

I like to keep a bed of soil around trees, when they are young, in a grass orchard (1). Mice can cause a good deal of damage to young trees by gnawing at the bark at ground level. If the bark is removed right round the stem the tree will usually die. They can be deterred by placing strips of sacking dipped in animal oil around the base of the stem (2).

When planting a standard tree I follow much the same procedure, but it is a job which is best done with two pairs of hands, one to hold the tree and shake it while soil is being returned (3). This shaking, together with adequate firming, ensures that the soil is in intimate contact with the roots so that fine fibrous feeding roots can form quickly. It is well worth spending a little extra time on providing adequate ties. In addition to the sacking round the stem I find it is worth putting a thick pad of sacking between stem and stake (4) and then tying firmly.

For the first few years after planting the pruning must be directed towards shaping the tree. Immediately after planting the leading shoots must be reduced by half their length. This and the removal of any blossom that is produced will give the tree a chance to settle down. Then, in later years, if the tree is of the kind which produces plenty of fruit buds and

spurs (short side growths) (these varieties include Cox's Orange Pippin, Allington Pippin, Lane's Prince Albert and other popular kinds) it is necessary to shorten side growths (1) in winter. This is known as spur pruning. Cut out also any dead wood and crossing branches (2) to leave the centre of the tree open.

A neglected tree needs drastic treatment (3). Saw out any branches coming from the base, making a cut below the branch first (4) and then sawing it right off close to the trunk (5). Paint the wounds over with white lead paint (6).

97

Large branches in the centre of the tree, particularly crossing branches, should be removed to open up the tree and admit more light and air, to enable the fruit to ripen properly. Use a saw for this job (1) and afterwards smooth off the cut surface by paring round the edge with a sharp knife (2 and 3). Paint the wounds over with Stockholm tar or lead paint to prevent the entry of disease organisms (4).

Areas of canker lesion should be cut away (1) and the area can be sealed over with a bituminous tree dressing (2).

Another system of winter pruning involves thinning out shoots to regulate growth. Cut out shoots that are rubbing together (3) or too close to each other (4), always removing the older shoot. Long extension growths are cut back to an outward pointing bud (5).

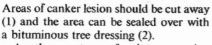

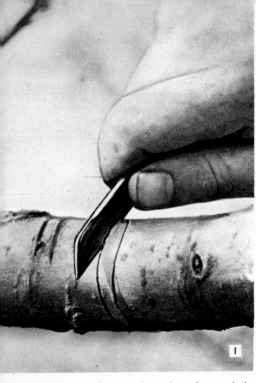

Trees sometimes make a lot of growth but fail to bear properly. If other methods of pruning have failed to curb vigour and bring the trees into bearing bark ringing can be tried at blossom time. Remove a thin ring of bark from the trunk or branch, using a sharp knife (1). Cut away the bark (2) and then cover the wound with several turns of adhesive tape (3 and 4). Never take a ring more than $\frac{1}{2}$ inch wide and on younger trees it should be about $\frac{1}{4}$ inch.

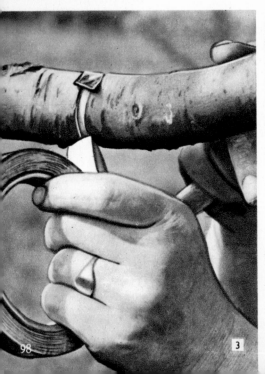

The young growths sometimes produced by cherry trees on the main stem must be removed (1) in spring or summer.

Cordon grown apple trees need summer pruning by cutting back the new side growths in late July to 5 leaves from the basal leaf cluster (2).

Apples need thinning after the June drop. Remove the 'king' or central apple first, together with any small or mis-shapen fruits (3). Leave one or two only on each cluster to develop.

Caterpillar damage (4) can be checked by spraying in spring with BHC. Remove and burn any fruits affected by brown rot (5).

A spray with tar-oil wash in winter (1) when apple trees are dormant, will clean them of moss and lichen and kill many over-wintering pests. In spring (2) spraying with D D T and B H C at pink bud and green cluster stages will kill apple blossom weavils, aphids and caterpillars, and early in May, at petal fall stage, a spray with captan or lime sulphur at $\frac{1}{4}$ pint to 3 gallons of water will deal with apple scab disease. This can be repeated (3) in summer against scab, but avoid using lime sulphur on sulphur-shy varieties. Pick carefully (4) and store, eye-up, in boxes (5) in a place where the atmosphere is cool and the temperature even.

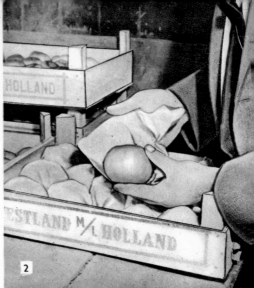

Apples in store should be inspected frequently (1) for signs of disease and any that show suspicious symptoms should be taken out and used immediately or discarded. Fruits will keep longer if wrapped in oiled paper wraps (2).

Apple shoots (scions) required for grafting in March are taken in winter and heeled in until required (3). The most popular method of top-grafting old trees is by rind-grafting. In this the branches are beheaded (4) and the stocks prepared by making vertical 2 inch long slits in the bark starting from the point of beheading. These are then opened with the end of a budding knife (5).

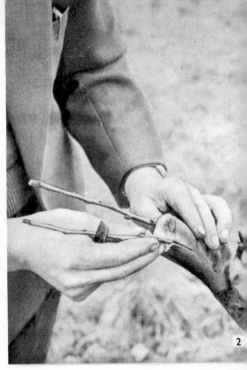

The scions are prepared by making 2 inch long slanting cuts on their lower ends (1). These ends are then inserted under the flaps of bark and pressed down until the slanting cuts are in close contact with the wood of the stock (2). The scions are then bound tightly in place with raffia (3) and the cut end of the stump and the raffia binding are covered thickly with grafting wax (4). Early in May loosen the ties if the branches have begun to swell. Rub off any shoots appearing below the grafts.

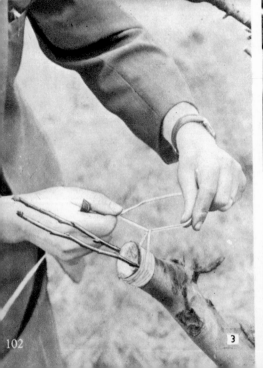

Eyed pins (1) are ideal for stretching wires over a wall surface for training fruit trees. At the end of each wire an adjustable bolt can be fixed so that the wire can be kept taut. Gauge 16 or 14 wire is best. The shoots of fan-trained trees, such as this Morello cherry (2), are tied into the wires to train them at the desired angle (3). After planting, surplus growths not required for training purposes are pruned away (4). Always prune to a bud. Instead of using eyed pins the wires can be secured to upright pieces of wood fixed to the wall at intervals of about 6 ft. At one end the wires can be nailed to the wooden upright and at the other end to adjustable bolts on the other wooden upright.

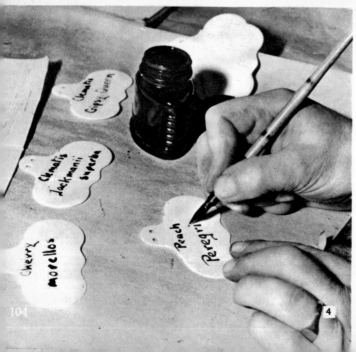

If the cherries set a heavy crop it pays to thin them. This is done either with a knife (1) or scissors. In late autumn prune unwanted growths, removing the old ones that have fruited (2) as morellos bear best on year-old laterals. At the same time it is necessary to go over the trees and tie in the new growths to stays in the wall (3) or to the wires. Preparing labels (4) is a good job for a wet day.

Wall-trained peaches (1) properly looked after yield delicious fruit. Spray in February with lime sulphur fungicide (2) to prevent peach leaf curl. To help the flowers set fruit go over them in early spring with a camel hair brush to transfer the pollen from flower to flower. Start disbudding in mid-April, rubbing out shoots growing towards the wall (3) and away from the wall. Retain those growing along the tops of branches. During spring and summer tie in new growths (4) to cover the wall evenly. Remember that the peach carries flowers and fruits on shoots made in the previous season. Spray against aphis in April, using malathion (5).

Wall-trained peaches often suffer from dryness at the roots so water well (1), particularly when the fruit is swelling. Between July and September go over the trees and remove surplus new growths (2). Tie in the young growths carefully (3 and 4) as these will bear fruit next year. This is a job that must be attended to constantly throughout the summer months. Feed the trees regularly, too, watering the fertiliser in. A heavy mulch of rotted manure or garden compost will provide additional food and retain moisture.

Suckers sometimes appear and they must be removed by digging down to the root from which they originate and pulling them off (1). Thinning of the fruitlets is done in two stages, first when the fruits are about the size of a cobnut (2) when the clusters should be reduced to singles, taking out all fruit near the wall and any that have insufficient room to develop properly (3). When the fruits begin to ripen expose them fully to the sun (4). A label tucked behind a fruit (5) will prevent leaves from shading it.

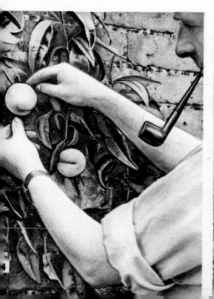

Old neglected wall-trained plums often need drastic pruning. Dead branches are sawn out (1). Branches affected by silver-leaf disease are cut out and burnt (2) as soon as they are seen. A dressing of sulphate of potash fertiliser in late winter (3) will help to encourage sturdy growth the following season. Afterwards mulch the ground round the trees with well-rotted manure or compost (4). The flowers appear early and, to protect them from frost, netting can be hung from the wall over the trees (5).

Established wall-trained plums need summer pruning and training. This consists in shortening new side growths (1) and tying in growths, required to extend the framework of branches (2).

Aphids can cause devastating damage on plums (3). Give regular precautionary sprays of BHC or malathion.

By mid-May apricot fruits should be partially thinned by removing a few fruits (4) and in June remove further fruits where they are overcrowded.

Wall-trained pears also need summer pruning. All the new shoots formed during the current year should be cut back to five or six leaves (1) in late July. It is very important to continue the training of trained trees and all new growths must be tied into the wires during the summer as they develop or after they are pruned (2). Where there is a heavy set of fruit (3) some thinning must be carried out to leave one or two fruits on each spur (4). Some varieties, such as Fertility, tend to produce a large number of small fruits but, if the fruits are thinned, fewer and larger fruits are produced.

In late summer tuck the leaves behind the fruits to bring them forward as an aid to ripening (1). When picking handle the fruits gently, cupping them in the hand and lifting them slightly (2). If they part easily from the stalk they are ripe. If not, leave them for a day or two longer. Burn any fruits affected by brown rot (3).

When raspberry canes arrive heel them in (4) until planting time. Plant in straight rows, making holes large enough to enable roots to be spread out properly (5).

After planting cut the canes down to within 6 inches of the ground (1). This is done to encourage strong growth from the roots. The new canes that are produced should fruit in the following year. In late winter give established plants a dressing of a good general fertiliser (2). Note the canes tied into their wires. A heavy mulch of strawy manure (3) is very helpful as it helps to keep the fine shallow roots moist. Tie in the canes to wires (4) stretched between stout posts. I use two wires fixed by straining bolts to the end posts. In February tip the canes at about 5 ft, just above the top wire (5).

Raspberries produce far too many new canes and they must be thinned (1) during the spring and summer to leave not more than eight to each stool. Spray with derris (2) ten days after blossoming and repeat ten days later, against raspberry beetle. Protect the fruits with netting or an old lace curtain (3) against the ravages of birds as the fruit ripens. After all fruit has been picked go over the bushes and cut out all the canes that have fruited (4) to leave the new canes well spaced out (5). These will fruit the following year.

Even the strongest of supporting posts rot in time and it is wise to inspect straining posts occassionally (1) for signs of rot at ground level. A row of raspberries in full leaf presents a good deal of wind resistance and the snapping of a post can be disastrous. Fork lightly between the rows after pruning (2), but remember that raspberries are surface-rooting so do not dig deeply. Hoe off any suckers coming up at a distance from the plants.

To propagate strawberry plants select the strongest runners in summer. Cut off their ends (3) beyond the small plants, sink small pots of potting compost in the soil near the plants (4) and peg the runners down into these with wire pins (5) bent to hairpin shape. Although sinking the

pots in the soil will help to keep them moist it is essential to look them over regularly in dry weather and water them if necessary (1). It is most convenient to plant the strawberries in straight rows, using a garden line as a guide and using a trowel for planting (2). Plant them in August so that the crown is level with the surface, no deeper. Spread the roots out on planting. In early spring fork between the plants (3) and scatter a general fertiliser or a special fruit fertiliser round the plants, but keep it off the leaves and crowns (4). Pick off any dead leaves at the same time. About the middle of May spread straw between the plants and tuck it under the leaves (5) to keep the fruit clean and away from the soil.

the ground. Examine fruits occasionally and remove any slug damaged specimens. Remove all unwanted runners as they develop (3).

When pruning gooseberries in late winter I cut the leading growths back to about half their length (4). This, together with the shortening of laterals, will encourage the formation of fruiting spurs. I also cut out old wood, weak growths and crossing branches to leave an open, goblet-shaped bush (5).

Instead of straw you can use mats (1). I net the plants in May against birds (2). These can be stretched over wires fixed to stakes about 2 ft. from

To stop birds from pecking out the buds in the winter I like to stretch black cotton or nylon thread between the shoots (1). A convenient method is to have the reel on the end of a stick. As a precaution against sawfly caterpillars, spray with derris (2) soon after the fruit has set. Some fruit can be picked when large enough for stewing (3) and the rest left to ripen for dessert. From the end of June plants can be summer pruned, reducing side shoots to about five leaves (4) to encourage fruit bud formation.

I like to give blackcurrant bushes plenty of room to develop so I never plant them closer than 5 ft. apart (1). After planting I cut them back hard to outward pointing buds and mulch them with rotted manure (2). An occasional spray with a suitable insecticide will prevent damage from greenfly (3). After the fruit has been picked I start pruning established bushes by cutting out the old stems that have borne fruit (4). This gives the new shoots, which will fruit next year, a chance to ripen better. The plants benefit from a dressing with a nitrogenous fertiliser applied in late July (5).

Vegetables and Salads

I have heard it said that vegetables are hardly worth growing because they are so cheap in the shops, but I do not agree with this. After all, apart from the satisfaction there is to be gained from growing good produce of your own for the kitchen, there can be no doubt that home-grown vegetables are fresher. In any case, by careful management and planning, it is possible to have garden crops ready for picking when they are very expensive in the shops. I agree that in small gardens it is not worth growing maincrop potatoes, for they take up so much room for such a long time, but it is certainly worth growing a few rows of earlies which can be cleared quickly and their room used for a follow-on crop.

The usual fault in most gardens is in having too much ready at once so that lettuces bolt, beans hang on the vines unpicked and radishes grow large and uneatable. But this is a fault that can be corrected quite easily by sowing little and often. Short rows of many vegetables and salads at intervals of every two or three weeks from March or April onwards will usually yield enough to feed the family without producing a glut. Some vegetables such as long beet, parsnips, maincrop carrots and onions can be grown for storage during the winter when they are sometimes expensive if not actually scarce.

Where space is limited I would be inclined to sow the less usual crops which are never cheap in the shops and are sometimes quite unobtainable. Among these I would include such salad crops as endive, which is much more than a substitute for lettuce in salads for, properly blanched, it introduces a new flavour. Chicory and seakale are two good vegetables that are always a little dear to buy. But they are easy enough to grow and blanch for use in winter and spring, especially if a greenhouse or warm cellar is available.

But, apart from growing the less common things, the amateur has a wonderful opportunity of growing the out-of-the-way varieties, particularly the varieties which suit his particular soil best. There is much room for experimenting here for it must be remembered that most commercial growers stick to the standard varieties which they know will give them heavy yields with the minimum of trouble. Unfortunately, it is true to say that these varieties are not always the kinds that have the best flavours. There are many kinds of vegetables available which may not give tremendous heads or roots but their taste is infinitely better than the kinds that are grown on the mass production system. Both yields and flavours vary with soils and it is always worth enquiring of local gardeners which kinds do best in that locality. That is one of the reasons why it is worth joining your local horticultural society.

Early in the year when the seed potatoes arrive I start them forming sprouts by standing them eye upwards in boxes (1). They are kept in cool but frost-proof conditions to produce short, sturdy, dark green or purplish sprouts. From mid-March onwards planting of earlies can begin. Before setting the seed potatoes in the drills I rub off surplus shoots (2) to leave two or three. After forking the plot over I like to take out a shallow v-shaped trench with a spade (3) into the bottom of which I scatter a good general fertiliser (4) followed by a layer of damp peat (5). The peat not only retains moisture but ensures clean tubers when the time comes to lift them. Instead of peat well decayed manure or garden compost can be used.

I plant my early potatoes a foot apart (1) in rows 2½ to 3 feet apart and cover them with 2 to 3 in. of soil, drawing it over them with a hoe (2). The process of earthing up is a gradual one which I like to start soon after the shoots appear through the soil. I draw the earth up with a hoe on either side of the row (3). From June onwards I spray with a copper fungicide against

potato blight (4). This can be very troublesome in a wet season and the foliage, if spraying is not carried out, will soon become blackened.

Lifting should be done carefully, using a fork, working well away from the plants to avoid damage to the tubers (5). With the earlies it is necessary only to lift a few roots at a time. Main crop tubers are lifted in September or October and stored in sacks in a frost-free shed (6).

Onion seed can be sown in heat in January, spacing the seed out in boxes (1) and covering them lightly with sifted soil (2). When the seedlings are large enough they can be removed from their boxes (3) and pricked out into boxes of potting compost, spacing them 2 in. apart (4)

and then watered (5).

I like to sow onion seed outdoors early in March or in early autumn on a very firm bed in which I have drawn shallow drills a foot apart with the hoe (6). The soil has been broken down to form a fine tilth. When large enough the seedlings are thinned (7) and the thinnings used in salads.

I transplant autumn-sown onions in late February to their permanent beds. These should be of firm, rich soil in a sunny, open position. Transplant 8 inches apart in rows 15 inches asunder (1). I hoe between the rows from time to time to keep weeds down (2) and dust with

aldrin or 4% calomel dust against onion fly (3). A little general fertiliser sprinkled along the rows (4) during the summer will encourage sturdy growth. In late July the leaves are bent over to assist ripening (5) and in August the bulbs are lifted and left on top of the soil for a few days to ripen. Then clean them (6) and store by plaiting the dry leaves together in ropes (7) and hanging them up in a dry shed.

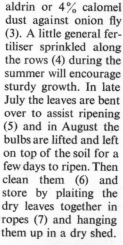

although before bad weather sets in it is a good plan to lift a few extra (5) and heel them in somewhere where they can easily be got at in frosty or snowy weather (6). Heeled in the soil in this way they will keep for many weeks

When planting leeks I make holes 6 to 8 inches deep and 9 inches apart with a dibber (1) and drop one leek in each hole (2) after dipping the ends in water to straighten the roots. Watering settles them in (3) and later, as the plants develop, I draw soil up around each plant (4) to get an extra long length of blanched stem. They can be lifted as needed from late autumn onwards,

Early in June I set out my young celery plants in prepared trenches of rich soil. I put the plants in about a foot apart (1) and then soak the trench. Before earthing up I remove all side growths (2). To get long, clean, blanched stems I tie the

shoots together (3) and put paper collars round the plants (4), then earth up (5). It is worth watering the trench with a slug killer before earthing up. In the autumn, as required, I dig round the plants (6), lift them out (7) and cut off the roots (8).

For an early crop I sow runner beans under glass towards the end of April. They are sown individually in small pots (1), covering the seeds with about an inch of compost (2). It is safe to sow outdoors by mid-May, in shallow trenches in rich, well-drained soil. I set the beans 8 inches apart in double rows 1 foot apart (3). For those sown under glass I prepare the bed by putting in stakes and when the plants are hardened off I set one beside each stake, using a trowel (4). A watering settles them in (5) and they soon get away. There are, of course, other ways of training beans apart from the method shown here. They can be grown up vertical stakes or up strings secured to a central pole in maypole fashion. A fine

spray each evening in dry weather helps to get a good set. To prevent the soil from drying out rapidly mulch the ground around the beans with compost.

It is best to pick frequently, when the beans are young and tender (1). In late autumn, after the last picking, some pods can be left on the plants for seed. When these are dry they are picked (2) and shelled (3). The beans are stored in labelled paper bags in a cool dry place until they are needed. After this the stakes can be taken up (4), stripped of the haulm and stood upside down (5) for use the following year, although before they are used again it is wise to examine them to see if they are sound.

Broad beans can be sown in deep boxes in the greenhouse in January and February, under cloches in January or in the open ground early in March. In mild districts longpod varieties can be sown in November. I sow the beans in wide drills 1½ inches deep in double rows, with 6 inches between beans and 18 inches between the double rows (1). After sowing and labelling the rows I draw soil over the beans with a rake (2). I keep the hoe going between the rows and plants to keep down weeds (3) and draw a little soil up round them in severe weather. It is important to stake against wind damage, using stout posts (4) connected by strings (5).

When the plants have set their first cluster of beans I pinch out the growing points (1) to encourage the beans to develop and to lessen the chances of attack by blackfly. I pick the beans when they are young from each plant (2) to give the others a chance to develop.

Seed of maincrop carrots is sown from mid-April onwards but however thinly one sows it is always necessary to thin the plants, singling them to 4 inches apart (3). The roots should be lifted in late September (4) before they split and stored in deep boxes of fairly dry sand or ashes. I put the carrots in the boxes in layers (5), covering each layer with sand or ashes. In this way they will keep through the winter.

Parsnips like a long season of growth and light soil that has been dug deeply. Ground that was manured well for a previous crop is best and fresh manure must not be used. Prior to sowing National Growmore fertiliser can be applied at 2 oz. per sq. yd. I aim to get the seed in by the end of February or early March. To save time in thinning I sow three or four seeds together in drills at 9 to 12 inch intervals (1). These are later singled, leaving the strongest plant (2). Cultivate between the rows (3) to keep them clear of weeds. In the autumn the roots are lifted carefully to avoid stabbing them (4). A convenient way of storing them is to build clamps in a sheltered place. I start by making a circle of roots. On these I pile dryish sand (5) and then build up the clamp with alternate layers of parsnips and sand.

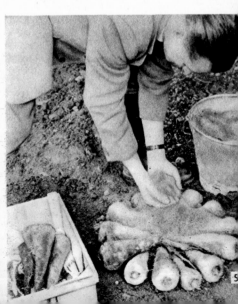

Beetroot is sown in succession from April onwards, but however thinly one sows the seedlings must always be thinned (1), leaving the strongest plant. For use in summer salads lift the roots as required and twist off the leaves (2). Maincrop roots can be left in the ground in mild counties for use when required or they can be lifted and stored in the same

way as carrots as shown on page 129, or clamped as shown on the opposite page.

Cabbage and other brassicas are sown from late February onwards in drills taken out with the hoe (3). Sow thinly (4) and shuffle soil back into the drills with the feet (5). A final rake over (6) will leave the seed bed tidy and remove footmarks. Always label the rows as you go along.

131

Dust along the rows of brassica seedlings occasionally with DDT to ward off attacks by flea-beetles (1). The plants need lifting (2) and transplanting later on to their permanent beds which should be well dug and reasonably rich Brussels sprouts in particular need a long season of growth and should be planted out by mid-May at the latest. Dip roots in a paste of 4% calomel dust and water (3), to prevent serious trouble from club root disease, before transplanting with a trowel (4). Draw up the earth round spring cabbage as winter approaches (5) to give them extra support.

After severe frosts it is worth going over
the cabbage plot and refirming plants
which have been lifted (1). Spring cabbage
benefit from a feed with a nitrogenous fertiliser in February (2). Cut the cabbages
as they mature (3).

Winter greens benefit from a feed in
early autumn (4), scattering the fertiliser
round the plants. Savoy cabbages (5) are
at their best in November and should be
cut and used in preference to the Brussels
sprouts which can well be left a little
longer.

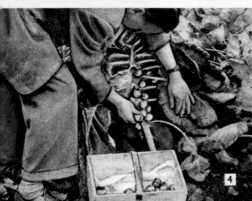

In late July I like to draw some earth up to the stems of Brussels sprouts (1) just as potatoes are earthed up. A topdressing of a compound fertiliser (2) a few weeks later will keep them growing steadily. In the autumn remove any yellowing leaves (3). Picking can usually start in late November, starting at the bottom of the stem and taking the largest "buttons" first (4). When all the sprouts have been picked do not forget that the tops of the plants are useful as a winter vegetable.

When the curds form on cauliflowers (5) I like to turn the leaves inwards (6) to protect the curds from the weather and keep them white.

Cut the shoots of sprouting broccoli (7) before the flower buds start to open.

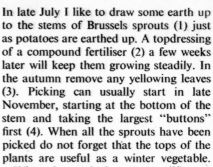

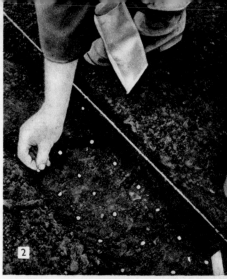

To get an early start with peas I sow them in pots in the greenhouse early in February, three or four in each $3\frac{1}{2}$-inch pot (1). This is a worthwhile practice in northern or other cold districts. Wrinkled-seeded varieties should be used for sowing under glass and it is important to grow the plants without much heat to ensure that they grow sturdily. Planting out can be done in late March in a warm and sheltered border after the plants have been hardened off. Outdoor sowings can start in late February in sheltered gardens, using round-seeded varieties. Sow in wide, shallow trenches in triple rows, spacing the seed 2 inches apart each way (2), and covering the seed with 2 inches of soil (3). Staking with twiggy pea-sticks should start quite early (4). After putting the sticks in place I shear the tops off evenly (5).

In dry weather spray or dust with BHC against attacks by pea thrips (1). These small insects cause distortion and a silvering of the pods. Dusting with DDT (2) 10 days after flowering begins will also protect against pea maggots.

To ensure regular supplies of lettuce I sow at intervals from late February onwards in shallow drills (3) drawn with the hoe, 12 inches apart (4). I shuffle soil back over the seeds with my feet (5) and tidy up the plot with a final rake over to remove footmarks.

Lettuce seedlings must be thinned out (1) as soon as they are large enough to handle, leaving them 1 foot apart. Winter lettuces benefit from a dressing with a quick-acting fertiliser in February or March (2). I use sulphate of ammonia but it must be kept off the leaves and hoed in afterwards. Go over winter lettuce plants occasionally and remove decaying leaves (3) to prevent the spread of disease. Keep a close watch for greenfly which often affects lettuce in early spring. Hoe between plants to keep down weeds (4).

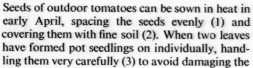

Seeds of outdoor tomatoes can be sown in heat in early April, spacing the seeds evenly (1) and covering them with fine soil (2). When two leaves have formed pot seedlings on individually, handling them very carefully (3) to avoid damaging the

tender stems. Grow the plants in a light position in the greenhouse where the temperature does not fall below 55.°

In the ring culture method I fill bottomless pots with John Innes potting compost standing on 6 inch deep beds of gravel or cinders (4). I then set one plant in each pot (5). Here they are being grown out of doors.

I set a bamboo cane in each bottomless cylinder (1) and tie the plants to the canes with raffia (2). When plants are grown by this method watering is done into the gravel or cinder base once the roots have penetrated into this (3).

Feeding is done into the bottomless pots (4). I like to give the plants a weekly feed with a good general fertiliser. The plants are stopped when four trusses of fruit have been formed (5) by removing the tip of the main stem.

Outdoor tomatoes can be set out in late May or early June. I plant them 18 inches apart (1) against bamboo canes, firming the plants (2) and tying them (3) both as soon as they are planted and as they develop. An important routine job is the removal of side shoots (4) as they appear, in order to keep the plants to a single stem. I feed the plants weekly, once two trusses have formed, with a good tomato fertiliser (5), applied in a ring round the stem. As tomatoes are members of the potato family they are liable to be infected with potato blight and in order to prevent this I give a routine spray with a copper fungicide (6). As it is not usually possible to ripen more than four trusses of fruit in the open the plants should be stopped in early August.

1

2

3

When growing marrows it is unwise to rely on insect pollination of the female flowers (those with embryo marrows behind the flower). It is necessary to dust these with the pollen from a male flower (1) to ensure that marrows will be produced. Keep the plants well supplied with water and feed occasionally with liquid manure. As the marrows develop I like to put a sheet of glass under them (2) to keep them off the soil. When ripe cut them with a piece of stem (3) and in the Autumn hang them up in nets if they are to be stored (4).

I plant cucumbers in frames towards the end of May on mounds of rich soil (5). Soon afterwards the plants are stopped by pinching out the growing point (6).

4

5

6

replanted in a new bed of moist, rich soil. The plants are lifted in the spring and split up into small pieces (4). Only the vigorous outside pieces should be used for planting. These pieces are replanted 9 inches apart (5) in rows 12 inches apart or in a shady corner where the soil is moist.

Stopping the plants will make them produce lateral growths, four of which I allow to develop. These I train to the four corners of the frame. Maintain a warm, moist atmosphere but give some ventilation on very hot days (1). Shade the glass to prevent the sun from scorching the plants. Cut the cucumbers regularly as they attain a reasonable size (2).

Mint can easily be forced by lifting some roots in Autumn and bringing them into the greenhouse where they are replanted in boxes of old potting soil. If they are kept moist and warm they will quickly produce new growths for use during the winter. Discard plants after forcing.

After a few years in the same bed mint in the open should be lifted (3) and

Melons are not difficult to grow in frames. They like much the same conditions as frame cucumbers. I plant them out singly in beds of rich soil (1) in late May. The fruits are produced on side-shoots and I allow four per plant to develop, stopping these when they reach the next plant or the corner of the frame (2). Allow one fruit only to develop on each lateral, remove all other flowers and be careful to pollinate all the female flowers on the same day if possible (3). Shade the frames in very sunny weather and allow some air (4). While the fruits ripen maintain a warm, moist atmosphere, not too stuffy. Cut when melon fragrance develops.

Asparagus is often grown on raised beds although it can conveniently be grown in rows on the flat. Each spring I like to rake off the top few inches of old soil from the beds (1) and apply a heavy topdressing of well-rotted manure (2). In March I give a dressing of salt at 1 oz. to the square yard (3). I cut the succulent young shoots when they are 3 or 4 inches tall, severing them with a knife well below the soil level (4). Cutting should finish by mid-June to allow the plants to make top growth.

Chicory is a succulent winter salad crop not grown often enough in my opinion. Seed is sown thinly in early June in $\frac{1}{2}$ inch deep drills. Seedlings are thinned to 9 inches apart and the rows kept hoed. By October good roots will have formed and these are dug up (1) and the outer leaves removed (2), leaving the inner, pale green or white leaves. I then twist off the tops of these (3) and lay the roots flat in a special sand bed (4).

I cover the chicory roots with sand (1) and leave them until they are needed for forcing from late November onwards. Roots are taken out of the sand as required, their bottoms are cut off (2) and they are packed in large pots with some old potting soil (3). Another flower pot is inverted

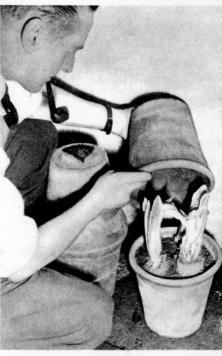

over them (4). To exclude light the drainage hole is covered. They force best in a warm greenhouse, shed or cellar. After a few weeks the thick shoots are blanched and can be broken off at ground level. Discard the roots after forcing.

Seakale is also forced in the winter. It can be grown from seed sown outdoors in April, when it takes two years to get roots large enough to lift, or from root cuttings. Whichever method is chosen the roots are lifted in autumn (1), the side roots cut off to provide cuttings for new stock (2), the tops of the leaves removed and the crown trimmed up (3). The crowns are stored in sand (4 and 5) in the same way as chicory roots shown here with the seakale crowns. The side roots I am holding (4) are bundled together and stored in sand until needed for root cuttings in spring. They should be 4 to 6 inches long and about the thickness of a pencil.

Seakale thongs to be used for making root cuttings are cut with a straight cut across their tops and a slanting cut along their bases (1) to ensure that they are put in right side up. They can be stored for the winter in pots of sandy soil (2) and planted outside in early April. By this time buds will have formed at the top of the cuttings and all but the strongest should be removed. Forcing of the crowns begins in December in batches. The crowns are put in large pots of old potting compost (3 and 4) and another flower pot is inverted over them (5), its drainage hole covered to obscure light. Forcing can be done in a greenhouse or shed with a temperature of 55°. Blanched shoots will be ready for cutting when they are 6 to 8 inches long. Discard the roots after forcing.

Endive is a crop that can be blanched for use in summer or winter salads. The seed is sown from April onwards and the seedlings thinned to 9 inches apart. Little attention is needed except for hoeing between the rows and dressing the soil with nitrate of soda. When the plants are well grown they can be blanched by inverting a flower pot over them (1 and 2). Exclude all light by placing a tile over the drainage hole (3). Leave them until the leaves are white (4), which takes about 5 weeks. They can then be cut for use in salads instead of lettuce.

Overgrown rhubarb clumps can be lifted in February or March (5) and divided up (6) with a spade for replanting in well prepared ground that is free of perennial weeds.

The pieces of rhubarb crown are replanted firmly in rich soil 3 or 4 feet apart (1), with their shoots just out of the soil. They are topdressed with rotted manure (3). Do not pull any sticks the first year and a few only in the second. Keep the plants watered well and mulch from time to time with rotted manure or compost. Cut off any flower spikes that develop (2).

Winter supplies of parsley can be obtained by carefully lifting a few young plants in October (4) and transferring them to a frame (5), planting them firmly (6).

I like to get an early start with crops by using cloches. On a dryish day in January the ground, which should be fertile and in a sheltered position, is prepared by forking it over, treading (1) and raking (2) to obtain a fine tilth. Drills are taken out in the normal way with a draw hoe (3), but can be closer together to get three rows under the normal barn cloche. In sheltered districts a start can be made in late January with lettuce, carrots, broad beans, round-seeded peas, onions and radishes, but it is best to wait for a month in cold districts. After sowing (4), the cloches are put in position over the rows (5).

Glass end pieces are put in position to close the ends of the row (1). In mild weather it is essential to take precautions against mice and slugs by putting down bait (2).

An early start can be obtained with outdoor tomatoes by planting them out under cloches in April (3). A double row can be accommodated under large barn cloches (4). By late May when the plants are getting too big for the cloches the glass can be taken off for the danger of frost will be over.

INDEX

A

Aerating, lawns, 14
Aldrin, 123
Alpines, planting, 27-28
  propagating, 28
Alyssum, planting, 29
Anenome-centred dahlias, 32
Annuals, sowing, 20
Aphides, 100, 109
Apple Blossom Weevil, 100
  scab, 100
Apples, grafting, 101-102
  picking, 100
  pruning, 95
    cordon, 99
  storing, 101
  thinning, 99
Apricots, fruits, thinning, 109
Asparagus, topdressing, 144
  cutting, 144
  feeding, 144
Aubrieta, planting, 29
Azaleas, planting, 79

B

Bark ringing, 98
Basic slag, 44
Baskets, hanging, 71-72
Beans, Broad, culture of, 128-129
  picking, 129
  pinching out, 129
  sowing, 128
  staking, 128
  under cloches, 151
Beans, Runner, seed saving, 127
  sowing, outdoors, 126
    under glass, 126
  picking, 127
  staking, 126
  watering, 126
Bedding, fuchias, 69
  plants, cultivation of, 56-72
    planting, 66, 67-69
    sowing, 57-58
    summer, clearing, 67
Beech hedge, 87
Beetroot, lifting, 131
  sowing, 131
  storing, 131
  thinning, 131

BHC
BHC, 45, 55, 109, 136
Birds, 68, 113, 116
Blackcurrants, feeding, 118
  mulching, 118
  spraying, 118
Blackfly, 129
Blanching, endive, 149
Blanket weed, 73, 74
Blight, potato, 121, 140
Blueing, hydrangeas, 80
Borders, flower, 19-24
Brassicas, sowing, 131
  winter, feeding, 133
  transplanting, 132
Broccoli, sprouting, 134
Brown Rot, 99, 111
Brussels sprouts, 132
  earthing up, 134
  picking, 134
  planting, 132
Buddleia davidii, 90
  pruning, 81
Butterfly-flowered gladioli, 38

C

Cabbages, cutting, 133
  feeding, 133
  sowing, 131
  spring, earthing up, 132
Cactus dahlias, 32
Calomel dust, 123
  paste, 132
Campanulas, planting, 29
Canker, 97
Cannas, lifting, 64
Carnations, Border, disbudding, 22
  planting, 22
Carrots, lifting, 129
  sowing, 129
  storing, 129
  under cloches, 151
Caryopteris clandonensis, pruning, 83
Caterpillars, 99, 100
Cauliflowers, protection of, 134
Celery, earthing up, 125
  planting, 125
Centaurea gymnocarpa,
  cultivation of, 65
  propagation of, 65-66
Chamaecyparis lawsoniana, hedge, 87

153

INDEX

INDEX